PostgreSQL Reference Manual

Volume 3: Server Administration Guide
for version 8.2.4.
June 2007

The PostgreSQL Global Development Group

Published by Network Theory Ltd.

A catalogue record for this book is available from the British Library.

First Printing, June 2007 (7/6/2007)

Published by Network Theory Limited.

15 Royal Park
Bristol
BS8 3AL
United Kingdom

Email: info@network-theory.co.uk

ISBN 0-9546120-4-3

Further information about this book is available from
http://www.network-theory.co.uk/postgresql/

This book has an unconditional guarantee. If you are not fully satisfied with
your purchase for any reason, please contact the publisher at the address above.

Table of Contents

Publisher's Preface

This volume is part of the official reference documentation for the PostgreSQL database management system.

PostgreSQL (pronounced "Postgres-Q-L") is a powerful database system with a long history, going back over 20 years to the POSTGRES project at the University of California at Berkeley. Today it provides a high level of conformance with the ANSI-SQL 92/99 standards and is fully ACID compliant.

In addition to its technical strengths, PostgreSQL offers a fundamental advantage over proprietary database software: the complete source code to PostgreSQL is available to everyone under a free software license, so users are not reliant on a single company to fix problems with it. Free software removes the single point of failure that exists when one company owns and controls a program.

To support the ongoing development of PostgreSQL, we will donate $1 to the PostgreSQL project for each copy of this book sold.

Brian Gough
Publisher
June 2007

Server Administration

This volume covers topics that are of interest to a PostgreSQL database administrator. This includes installation of the software, set up and configuration of the server, management of users and databases, and maintenance tasks. Anyone who runs a PostgreSQL server, even for personal use, but especially in production, should be familiar with the topics covered in this volume.

The information in this volume is arranged approximately in the order in which a new user should read it, but the chapters are self-contained and can be read individually as desired. Readers looking for a complete description of a particular command should look into the SQL Command Reference (Volume 1).

The first few chapters are written so that they can be understood without prerequisite knowledge, so that new users who need to set up their own server can begin their exploration with this volume. The rest of this volume is about tuning and management; that material assumes that the reader is familiar with the general use of the PostgreSQL database system. Readers are encouraged to look at Volume 1 for additional information.

1 Installation Instructions

This chapter describes the installation of PostgreSQL from the source code distribution. (If you are installing a pre-packaged distribution, such as an RPM or Debian package, ignore this chapter and read the packager's instructions instead.)

1.1 Short Version

```
./configure
gmake
su
gmake install
adduser postgres
mkdir /usr/local/pgsql/data
chown postgres /usr/local/pgsql/data
su - postgres
/usr/local/pgsql/bin/initdb -D /usr/local/pgsql/data
/usr/local/pgsql/bin/postgres -D /usr/local/pgsql/data
 >logfile 2>&1 &
/usr/local/pgsql/bin/createdb test
/usr/local/pgsql/bin/psql test
```

The long version is the rest of this chapter.

1.2 Requirements

In general, a modern Unix-compatible platform should be able to run PostgreSQL. The platforms that had received specific testing at the time of release are listed in Section 1.7 *Supported Platforms*, page 19 below. In the 'doc' sub-directory of the distribution there are several platform-specific FAQ documents you might wish to consult if you are having trouble.

The following software packages are required for building PostgreSQL:

- GNU make is required; other make programs will *not* work. GNU make is often installed under the name 'gmake'; this document will always refer to it by that name. (On some systems GNU make is the default tool with the name 'make'.) To test for GNU make enter

  ```
  gmake --version
  ```

  It is recommended to use version 3.76.1 or later.

- You need an ISO/ANSI C compiler. Recent versions of GCC are recommendable, but PostgreSQL is known to build with a wide variety of compilers from different vendors.

- tar is required to unpack the source distribution in the first place, in addition to either gzip or bzip2.

- The GNU Readline library (for simple line editing and command history re-
  trieval) is used by default. If you don't want to use it then you must specify
  the --without-readline option for 'configure'. As an alternative, you
  can often use the BSD-licensed 'libedit' library, originally developed on
  NetBSD. The 'libedit' library is GNU Readline-compatible and is used if
  'libreadline' is not found, or if --with-libedit-preferred is used as an
  option to 'configure'. If you are using a package-based GNU/Linux distribution, be aware that you need both the readline and readline-devel
  packages, if those are separate in your distribution.

- The zlib compression library will be used by default. If you don't want to
  use it then you must specify the --without-zlib option for 'configure'.
  Using this option disables support for compressed archives in pg_dump
  and pg_restore.

- Additional software is needed to build PostgreSQL on Windows. You can
  build PostgreSQL for NT-based versions of Windows (like Windows XP
  and 2003) using MinGW; see 'doc/FAQ_MINGW' for details. You can also
  build PostgreSQL using Cygwin; see 'doc/FAQ_CYGWIN'. A Cygwin-based
  build will work on older versions of Windows, but if you have a choice,
  we recommend the MinGW approach. While these are the only tool sets
  recommended for a complete build, it is possible to build just the C client
  library (libpq) and the interactive terminal (psql) using other Windows
  tool sets. For details of that see Chapter 2 *Client-Only Installation on
  Windows*, page 25.

The following packages are optional. They are not required in the default
configuration, but they are needed when certain build options are enabled, as
explained below.

- To build the server programming language PL/Perl you need a full Perl
  installation, including the 'libperl' library and the header files. Since
  PL/Perl will be a shared library, the 'libperl' library must be a shared
  library also on most platforms. This appears to be the default in recent
  Perl versions, but it was not in earlier versions, and in any case it is the
  choice of whomever installed Perl at your site.

  If you don't have the shared library but you need one, a message like this
  will appear during the build to point out this fact:

  ```
  *** Cannot build PL/Perl because libperl is not a
  *** shared library. You might have to rebuild your
  *** Perl installation. Refer to the documentation for
  *** details.
  ```

  (If you don't follow the on-screen output you will merely notice that the
  PL/Perl library object, 'plperl.so' or similar, will not be installed.) If
  you see this, you will have to rebuild and install Perl manually to be able
  to build PL/Perl. During the configuration process for Perl, request a
  shared library.

- To build the PL/Python server programming language, you need a Python installation with the header files and the distutils module. The distutils module is included by default with Python 1.6 and later; users of earlier versions of Python will need to install it.

  Since PL/Python will be a shared library, the 'libpython' library must be a shared library also on most platforms. This is not the case in a default Python installation. If after building and installing you have a file called 'plpython.so' (possibly a different extension), then everything went well. Otherwise you should have seen a notice like this flying by:

  ```
  *** Cannot build PL/Python because libpython is not a
  *** shared library. You might have to rebuild your
  *** Python installation. Refer to the documentation
  *** for details.
  ```

  That means you have to rebuild (part of) your Python installation to supply this shared library.

  If you have problems, run Python 2.3 or later's configure using the --enable-shared flag. On some operating systems you don't have to build a shared library, but you will have to convince the PostgreSQL build system of this. Consult the 'Makefile' in the 'src/pl/plpython' directory for details.

- If you want to build the PL/Tcl procedural language, you of course need a Tcl installation.

- To enable Native Language Support (NLS), that is, the ability to display a program's messages in a language other than English, you need an implementation of the Gettext API. Some operating systems have this built-in (e.g., Linux, NetBSD, Solaris), for other systems you can download an add-on gettext package.[1] If you are using the Gettext implementation in the GNU C library then you will additionally need the GNU Gettext package for some utility programs. For any of the other implementations you will not need it.

- Kerberos, OpenSSL, OpenLDAP, and/or PAM, if you want to support authentication or encryption using these services.

If you are building from a CVS tree instead of using a released source package, or if you want to do development, you also need the following packages:

- GNU Flex and Bison are needed to build a CVS checkout or if you changed the actual scanner and parser definition files. If you need them, be sure to get Flex 2.5.4 or later and Bison 1.875 or later. Other yacc programs can sometimes be used, but doing so requires extra effort and is not recommended. Other lex programs will definitely not work.

---

[1] Available from http://developer.postgresql.org/~petere/bsd-gettext/.

If you need to get a GNU package, you can find it at your local GNU mirror site[2] or at `ftp://ftp.gnu.org/gnu/`.

Also check that you have sufficient disk space. You will need about 65 MB for the source tree during compilation and about 15 MB for the installation directory. An empty database cluster takes about 25 MB, databases take about five times the amount of space that a flat text file with the same data would take. If you are going to run the regression tests you will temporarily need up to an extra 90 MB. Use the `df` command to check free disk space.

1.3 Getting The Source

The PostgreSQL 8.2.4 sources can be obtained by anonymous FTP from `ftp.postgresql.org`.[3] Other download options can be found on our website: `http://www.postgresql.org/download/`. After you have obtained the file, unpack it:

```
gunzip postgresql-8.2.4.tar.gz
tar xf postgresql-8.2.4.tar
```

This will create a directory 'postgresql-8.2.4' under the current directory with the PostgreSQL sources. Change into that directory for the rest of the installation procedure.

1.4 If You Are Upgrading

The internal data storage format changes with new releases of PostgreSQL. Therefore, if you are upgrading an existing installation that does not have a version number "8.2.x", you must back up and restore your data as shown here. These instructions assume that your existing installation is under the '/usr/local/pgsql' directory, and that the data area is in '/usr/local/pgsql/data'. Substitute your paths appropriately.

1. Make sure that your database is not updated during or after the backup. This does not affect the integrity of the backup, but the changed data would of course not be included. If necessary, edit the permissions in the file '/usr/local/pgsql/data/pg_hba.conf' (or equivalent) to disallow access from everyone except you.

2. To back up your database installation, type:

   ```
   pg_dumpall > outputfile
   ```

   If you need to preserve OIDs (such as when using them as foreign keys), then use the -o option when running pg_dumpall.

   To make the backup, you can use the pg_dumpall command from the version you are currently running. For best results, however, try to use the pg_dumpall command from PostgreSQL 8.2.4, since this version contains bug fixes and improvements over older versions. While this advice might seem idiosyncratic since you haven't installed the new version yet, it is

---

[2] See `http://www.gnu.org/order/ftp.html` for a list.

[3] `ftp://ftp.postgresql.org/pub/source/v8.2.4/postgresql-8.2.4.tar.gz`

advisable to follow it if you plan to install the new version in parallel with the old version. In that case you can complete the installation normally and transfer the data later. This will also decrease the downtime.

3. If you are installing the new version at the same location as the old one then shut down the old server, at the latest before you install the new files:

   ```
   pg_ctl stop
   ```

   On systems that have PostgreSQL started at boot time, there is probably a start-up file that will accomplish the same thing. For example, on a Red Hat system one might find that

   ```
   /etc/rc.d/init.d/postgresql stop
   ```

   works.

4. If you are installing in the same place as the old version then it is also a good idea to move the old installation out of the way, in case you have trouble and need to revert to it. Use a command like this:

   ```
   mv /usr/local/pgsql /usr/local/pgsql.old
   ```

After you have installed PostgreSQL 8.2.4, create a new database directory and start the new server. Remember that you must execute these commands while logged in to the special database user account (which you already have if you are upgrading).

```
/usr/local/pgsql/bin/initdb -D /usr/local/pgsql/data
/usr/local/pgsql/bin/postgres -D /usr/local/pgsql/data
```

Finally, restore your data with

```
/usr/local/pgsql/bin/psql -d postgres -f outputfile
```

using the *new* psql.

Further discussion appears in Section 10.5 *Migration Between Releases*, page 149, which you are encouraged to read in any case.

1.5 Installation Procedure

1. **Configuration:**

   The first step of the installation procedure is to configure the source tree for your system and choose the options you would like. This is done by running the 'configure' script. For a default installation simply enter

   ```
   ./configure
   ```

   This script will run a number of tests to guess values for various system dependent variables and detect some quirks of your operating system, and finally will create several files in the build tree to record what it found. (You can also run 'configure' in a directory outside the source tree if you want to keep the build directory separate.)

   The default configuration will build the server and utilities, as well as all client applications and interfaces that require only a C compiler. All files will be installed under '/usr/local/pgsql' by default.

   You can customize the build and installation process by supplying one or more of the following command line options to 'configure':

`--prefix=PREFIX`
> Install all files under the directory *PREFIX* instead of
> '/usr/local/pgsql'. The actual files will be installed into various
> subdirectories; no files will ever be installed directly into the
> *PREFIX* directory.
>
> If you have special needs, you can also customize the individual sub-
> directories with the following options. However, if you leave these
> with their defaults, the installation will be relocatable, meaning you
> can move the directory after installation. (The man and doc locations
> are not affected by this.)
>
> For relocatable installs, you might want to use 'configure''s
> `--disable-rpath` option. Also, you will need to tell the operating
> system how to find the shared libraries.

`--exec-prefix=EXEC-PREFIX`
> You can install architecture-dependent files under a different prefix,
> *EXEC-PREFIX*, than what *PREFIX* was set to. This can be useful to
> share architecture-independent files between hosts. If you omit this,
> then *EXEC-PREFIX* is set equal to *PREFIX* and both architecture-
> dependent and independent files will be installed under the same tree,
> which is probably what you want.

`--bindir=DIRECTORY`
> Specifies the directory for executable programs. The default is '*EXEC-
> PREFIX*/bin', which normally means '/usr/local/pgsql/bin'.

`--datadir=DIRECTORY`
> Sets the directory for read-only data files used by the installed pro-
> grams. The default is '*PREFIX*/share'. Note that this has nothing to
> do with where your database files will be placed.

`--sysconfdir=DIRECTORY`
> The directory for various configuration files, '*PREFIX*/etc' by default.

`--libdir=DIRECTORY`
> The location to install libraries and dynamically loadable modules.
> The default is '*EXEC-PREFIX*/lib'.

`--includedir=DIRECTORY`
> The directory for installing C and C++ header files. The default is
> '*PREFIX*/include'.

`--mandir=DIRECTORY`
> The man pages that come with PostgreSQL will be installed under
> this directory, in their respective 'man*x*' subdirectories. The default
> is '*PREFIX*/man'.

`--with-docdir=`*`DIRECTORY`*
`--without-docdir`

> Documentation files, except "man" pages, will be installed into this directory. The default is '*PREFIX*/doc'. If the option `--without-docdir` is specified, the documentation will not be installed by `make install`. This is intended for packaging scripts that have special methods for installing documentation.

> **Note:** Care has been taken to make it possible to install PostgreSQL into shared installation locations (such as '/usr/local/include') without interfering with the namespace of the rest of the system. First, the string "/postgresql" is automatically appended to `datadir`, `sysconfdir`, and `docdir`, unless the fully expanded directory name already contains the string "postgres" or "pgsql". For example, if you choose '/usr/local' as prefix, the documentation will be installed in '/usr/local/doc/postgresql', but if the prefix is '/opt/postgres', then it will be in '/opt/postgres/doc'. The public C header files of the client interfaces are installed into `includedir` and are namespace-clean. The internal header files and the server header files are installed into private directories under `includedir`. See the documentation of each interface for information about how to get at the its header files. Finally, a private subdirectory will also be created, if appropriate, under `libdir` for dynamically loadable modules.

`--with-includes=`*`DIRECTORIES`*

> *DIRECTORIES* is a colon-separated list of directories that will be added to the list the compiler searches for header files. If you have optional packages (such as GNU Readline) installed in a non-standard location, you have to use this option and probably also the corresponding `--with-libraries` option.

> Example: `--with-includes=/opt/gnu/include:/usr/sup/include`.

`--with-libraries=`*`DIRECTORIES`*

> *DIRECTORIES* is a colon-separated list of directories to search for libraries. You will probably have to use this option (and the corresponding `--with-includes` option) if you have packages installed in non-standard locations.

> Example: `--with-libraries=/opt/gnu/lib:/usr/sup/lib`.

`--enable-nls[=`*`LANGUAGES`*`]`

> Enables Native Language Support (NLS), that is, the ability to display a program's messages in a language other than English. *LANGUAGES* is a space-separated list of codes of the languages that you want supported, for example `--enable-nls='de fr'`. (The intersection between your list and the set of actually provided translations will be computed automatically.) If you do not specify a list, then all available translations are installed.

To use this option, you will need an implementation of the Gettext API; see above.

`--with-pgport=`*NUMBER*

Set *NUMBER* as the default port number for server and clients. The default is 5432. The port can always be changed later on, but if you specify it here then both server and clients will have the same default compiled in, which can be very convenient. Usually the only good reason to select a non-default value is if you intend to run multiple PostgreSQL servers on the same machine.

`--with-perl`

Build the PL/Perl server-side language.

`--with-python`

Build the PL/Python server-side language.

`--with-tcl`

Build the PL/Tcl server-side language.

`--with-tclconfig=`*DIRECTORY*

Tcl installs the file 'tclConfig.sh', which contains configuration information needed to build modules interfacing to Tcl. This file is normally found automatically at a well-known location, but if you want to use a different version of Tcl you can specify the directory in which to look for it.

`--with-krb5`

Build with support for Kerberos 5 authentication. On many systems, the Kerberos system is not installed in a location that is searched by default (e.g., '/usr/include', '/usr/lib'), so you must use the options `--with-includes` and `--with-libraries` in addition to this option. 'configure' will check for the required header files and libraries to make sure that your Kerberos installation is sufficient before proceeding.

`--with-krb-srvnam=`*NAME*

The default name of the Kerberos service principal. postgres is the default. There's usually no reason to change this.

`--with-openssl`

Build with support for SSL (encrypted) connections. This requires the OpenSSL package to be installed. 'configure' will check for the required header files and libraries to make sure that your OpenSSL installation is sufficient before proceeding.

`--with-pam`

Build with PAM (Pluggable Authentication Modules) support.

`--with-ldap`

> Build with LDAP support for authentication and connection parameter lookup (see Volume 2, Section 1.15 *LDAP Lookup of Connection Parameters* and Section 7.2.5 *LDAP authentication*, page 109 for more information). On Unix, this requires the OpenLDAP package to be installed. 'configure' will check for the required header files and libraries to make sure that your OpenLDAP installation is sufficient before proceeding. On Windows, the default WinLDAP library is used.

`--without-readline`

> Prevents use of the Readline library (and libedit as well). This option disables command-line editing and history in psql, so it is not recommended.

`--with-libedit-preferred`

> Favors the use of the BSD-licensed libedit library rather than GPL-licensed Readline. This option is significant only if you have both libraries installed; the default in that case is to use Readline.

`--with-bonjour`

> Build with Bonjour support. This requires Bonjour support in your operating system. Recommended on Mac OS X.

`--enable-integer-datetimes`

> Use 64-bit integer storage for datetimes and intervals, rather than the default floating-point storage. This reduces the range of representable values but guarantees microsecond precision across the full range (see Volume 1, Section 6.5 *Date/Time Types* for more information). Note also that the integer datetimes code is newer than the floating-point code, and we still find bugs in it from time to time.

`--disable-spinlocks`

> Allow the build to succeed even if PostgreSQL has no CPU spinlock support for the platform. The lack of spinlock support will result in poor performance; therefore, this option should only be used if the build aborts and informs you that the platform lacks spinlock support. If this option is required to build PostgreSQL on your platform, please report the problem to the PostgreSQL developers.

`--enable-thread-safety`

> Make the client libraries thread-safe. This allows concurrent threads in libpq and ECPG programs to safely control their private connection handles. This option requires adequate threading support in your operating system.

`--without-zlib`

> Prevents use of the Zlib library. This disables support for compressed archives in pg_dump and pg_restore. This option is only intended for those rare systems where this library is not available.

`--enable-debug`
>   Compiles all programs and libraries with debugging symbols. This means that you can run the programs through a debugger to analyze problems. This enlarges the size of the installed executables considerably, and on non-GCC compilers it usually also disables compiler optimization, causing slowdowns. However, having the symbols available is extremely helpful for dealing with any problems that may arise. Currently, this option is recommended for production installations only if you use GCC. But you should always have it on if you are doing development work or running a beta version.

`--enable-cassert`
>   Enables *assertion* checks in the server, which test for many "can't happen" conditions. This is invaluable for code development purposes, but the tests slow things down a little. Also, having the tests turned on won't necessarily enhance the stability of your server! The assertion checks are not categorized for severity, and so what might be a relatively harmless bug will still lead to server restarts if it triggers an assertion failure. Currently, this option is not recommended for production use, but you should have it on for development work or when running a beta version.

`--enable-depend`
>   Enables automatic dependency tracking. With this option, the makefiles are set up so that all affected object files will be rebuilt when any header file is changed. This is useful if you are doing development work, but is just wasted overhead if you intend only to compile once and install. At present, this option will work only if you use GCC.

`--enable-dtrace`
>   Compiles with support for the dynamic tracing tool DTrace. Operating system support for DTrace is currently only available in Solaris.
>
>   To point to the `dtrace` program, the environment variable `DTRACE` can be set. This will often be necessary because `dtrace` is typically installed under '/usr/sbin', which might not be in the path. Additional command-line options for the `dtrace` program can be specified in the environment variable `DTRACEFLAGS`.
>
>   To include DTrace support in a 64-bit binary, specify `DTRACEFLAGS="-64"` to configure.
>
>   For example, using the GCC compiler:

```
./configure CC='gcc -m64' --enable-dtrace
DTRACEFLAGS='-64' ...
```

>   Using Sun's compiler:

```
./configure CC='/opt/SUNWspro/bin/cc -xtarget=native64'
--enable-dtrace DTRACEFLAGS='-64' ...
```

If you prefer a C compiler different from the one 'configure' picks, you can set the environment variable CC to the program of your choice. By default, 'configure' will pick 'gcc' if available, else the platform's default (usually 'cc'). Similarly, you can override the default compiler flags if needed with the CFLAGS variable.

You can specify environment variables on the 'configure' command line, for example:

```
./configure CC=/opt/bin/gcc CFLAGS='-O2 -pipe'
```

Here is a list of the significant variables that can be set in this manner:

CC   C compiler

CFLAGS
> options to pass to the C compiler

CPP
> C preprocessor

CPPFLAGS
> options to pass to the C preprocessor

DTRACE
> location of the dtrace program

DTRACEFLAGS
> options to pass to the dtrace program

LDFLAGS
> options to pass to the link editor

LDFLAGS_SL
> linker options for shared library linking

MSGFMT
> msgfmt program for native language support

PERL
> Full path to the Perl interpreter. This will be used to determine the dependencies for building PL/Perl.

PYTHON
> Full path to the Python interpreter. This will be used to determine the dependencies for building PL/Python.

TCLSH
> Full path to the Tcl interpreter. This wil be used to determine the dependencies for building PL/Tcl.

YACC
> Yacc program (bison -y if using Bison)

2. **Build:**

To start the build, type

```
gmake
```

(Remember to use GNU make.) The build may take anywhere from 5 minutes to half an hour depending on your hardware. The last line displayed
should be

```
All of PostgreSQL is successfully made. Ready to install.
```

3. **Regression Tests:**

   If you want to test the newly built server before you install it, you can run
   the regression tests at this point. The regression tests are a test suite to
   verify that PostgreSQL runs on your machine in the way the developers
   expected it to. Type

   ```
   gmake check
   ```

   (This won't work as root; do it as an unprivileged user.) Chapter 15 *Regression Tests*, page 177 contains detailed information about interpreting
   the test results. You can repeat this test at any later time by issuing the
   same command.

4. **Installing The Files:**

   Note: If you are upgrading an existing system and are going
   to install the new files over the old ones, be sure to back up
   your data and shut down the old server before proceeding, as
   explained in Section 1.4 *If You Are Upgrading*, page 8 above.

   To install PostgreSQL enter

   ```
   gmake install
   ```

   This will install files into the directories that were specified in *Configuration*, page 9. Make sure that you have appropriate permissions to write
   into that area. Normally you need to do this step as root. Alternatively,
   you could create the target directories in advance and arrange for appropriate permissions to be granted.

   You can use gmake install-strip instead of gmake install to strip the
   executable files and libraries as they are installed. This will save some
   space. If you built with debugging support, stripping will effectively remove the debugging support, so it should only be done if debugging is no
   longer needed. install-strip tries to do a reasonable job saving space,
   but it does not have perfect knowledge of how to strip every unneeded
   byte from an executable file, so if you want to save all the disk space you
   possibly can, you will have to do manual work.

   The standard installation provides all the header files needed for client
   application development as well as for server-side program development,
   such as custom functions or data types written in C. (Prior to PostgreSQL
   8.0, a separate gmake install-all-headers command was needed for the
   latter, but this step has been folded into the standard install.)

   Client-only installation:. If you want to install only the client applications and interface libraries, then you can use these commands:

```
gmake -C src/bin install
gmake -C src/include install
gmake -C src/interfaces install
gmake -C doc install
```

'src/bin' has a few binaries for server-only use, but they are small.

Registering eventlog on Windows:. To register a Windows eventlog library with the operating system, issue this command after installation:

```
regsvr32 pgsql_library_directory/pgevent.dll
```

This creates registry entries used by the event viewer.

Uninstallation:. To undo the installation use the command gmake uninstall. However, this will not remove any created directories.

Cleaning:. After the installation you can make room by removing the built files from the source tree with the command gmake clean. This will preserve the files made by the configure program, so that you can rebuild everything with gmake later on. To reset the source tree to the state in which it was distributed, use gmake distclean. If you are going to build for several platforms within the same source tree you must do this and re-configure for each build. (Alternatively, use a separate build tree for each platform, so that the source tree remains unmodified.)

If you perform a build and then discover that your configure options were wrong, or if you change anything that configure investigates (for example, software upgrades), then it's a good idea to do gmake distclean before reconfiguring and rebuilding. Without this, your changes in configuration choices may not propagate everywhere they need to.

1.6 Post-Installation Setup

1.6.1 Shared Libraries

On some systems that have shared libraries (which most systems do) you need to tell your system how to find the newly installed shared libraries. The systems on which this is *not* necessary include BSD/OS, FreeBSD, HP-UX, IRIX, Linux, NetBSD, OpenBSD, Tru64 UNIX (formerly Digital UNIX), and Solaris.

The method to set the shared library search path varies between platforms, but the most widely usable method is to set the environment variable LD_LIBRARY_PATH like so: In Bourne shells (sh, ksh, bash, zsh)

```
LD_LIBRARY_PATH=/usr/local/pgsql/lib
export LD_LIBRARY_PATH
```

or in csh or tcsh

```
setenv LD_LIBRARY_PATH /usr/local/pgsql/lib
```

Replace /usr/local/pgsql/lib with whatever you set --libdir to in *Configuration*, page 9. You should put these commands into a shell start-up file such as '/etc/profile' or '~/.bash_profile'.

On some systems it might be preferable to set the environment variable LD_RUN_PATH *before* building.

On Cygwin, put the library directory in the PATH or move the '.dll' files into the 'bin' directory.

If in doubt, refer to the manual pages of your system (perhaps ld.so or rld). If you later on get a message like

```
psql: error in loading shared libraries
libpq.so.2.1: cannot open shared object file: No such file or
  directory
```

then this step was necessary. Simply take care of it then.

If you are on BSD/OS, Linux, or SunOS 4 and you have root access you can run

```
/sbin/ldconfig /usr/local/pgsql/lib
```

(or equivalent directory) after installation to enable the run-time linker to find the shared libraries faster. Refer to the manual page of ldconfig for more information. On FreeBSD, NetBSD, and OpenBSD the command is

```
/sbin/ldconfig -m /usr/local/pgsql/lib
```

instead. Other systems are not known to have an equivalent command.

1.6.2 Environment Variables

If you installed into '/usr/local/pgsql' or some other location that is not searched for programs by default, you should add '/usr/local/pgsql/bin' (or whatever you set --bindir to in *Configuration*, page 9) into your PATH. Strictly speaking, this is not necessary, but it will make the use of PostgreSQL much more convenient.

To do this, add the following to your shell start-up file, such as '~/.bash_profile' (or '/etc/profile', if you want it to affect every user):

```
PATH=/usr/local/pgsql/bin:$PATH
export PATH
```

If you are using csh or tcsh, then use this command:

```
set path = ( /usr/local/pgsql/bin $path )
```

To enable your system to find the man documentation, you need to add lines like the following to a shell start-up file unless you installed into a location that is searched by default.

```
MANPATH=/usr/local/pgsql/man:$MANPATH
export MANPATH
```

The environment variables PGHOST and PGPORT specify to client applications the host and port of the database server, overriding the compiled-in defaults. If you are going to run client applications remotely then it is convenient if every user that plans to use the database sets PGHOST. This is not required, however: the settings can be communicated via command line options to most client programs.

1.7 Supported Platforms

PostgreSQL has been verified by the developer community to work on the platforms listed below. A supported platform generally means that PostgreSQL builds and installs according to these instructions and that the regression tests pass. "Build farm" entries refer to active test machines in the PostgreSQL Build Farm[4]. Platform entries that show an older version of PostgreSQL are those that did not receive explicit testing at the time of release of version 8.2 but that we still expect to work.

> **Note:** If you are having problems with the installation on a supported platform, please write to pgsql-bugs@postgresql.org or pgsql-ports@postgresql.org, not to the people listed here.

OS	PROCESSOR	VERSION	NOTES
AIX	PowerPC	8.2.0	Build farm grebe (5.3, gcc 4.0.1); kookaburra (5.2, cc 6.0); asp (5.2, gcc 3.3.2) see 'doc/FAQ_AIX', particularly if using AIX 5.3 ML3
AIX	RS6000	8.0.0	Hans-Jürgen Schönig (hs@cybertec.at), 2004-12-06 see 'doc/FAQ_AIX'
BSD/OS	x86	8.1.0	Bruce Momjian (pgman@candle.pha.pa.us), 2005-10-26 4.3.1
Debian GNU/Linux	Alpha	8.2.0	Build farm hare (3.1, gcc 3.3.4)
Debian GNU/Linux	AMD64	8.2.0	Build farm shad (4.0, gcc 4.1.2); kite (3.1, gcc 4.0); panda (sid, gcc 3.3.5)
Debian GNU/Linux	ARM	8.2.0	Build farm penguin (3.1, gcc 3.3.4)
Debian GNU/Linux	Athlon XP	8.2.0	Build farm rook (3.1, gcc 3.3.5)
Debian GNU/Linux	IA64	8.2.0	Build farm dugong (unstable, icc 9.1.045)
Debian GNU/Linux	m68k	8.0.0	Noël Köthe (noel@debian.org), 2004-12-09 sid
Debian GNU/Linux	MIPS	8.2.0	Build farm otter (3.1, gcc 3.3.4)
Debian GNU/Linux	MIPSEL	8.2.0	Build farm lionfish (3.1, gcc 3.3.4); corgi (3.1, gcc 3.3.4)
Debian GNU/Linux	PA-RISC	8.2.0	Build farm manatee (3.1, gcc 4.0.1); kingfisher (3.1, gcc 3.3.5)
Debian GNU/Linux	PowerPC	8.0.0	Noël Köthe (noel@debian.org), 2004-12-15 sid

---

[4] http://buildfarm.postgresql.org/

Debian GNU/Linux	Sparc	8.1.0	Build farm dormouse (3.1, gcc 3.2.5; 64-bit)
Debian GNU/Linux	x86	8.2.0	Build farm wildebeest (3.1, gcc 3.3.5)
Fedora Linux	AMD64	8.2.0	Build farm impala (FC6, gcc 4.1.1); bustard (FC5, gcc 4.1.0); wasp (FC5, gcc 4.1.0); viper (FC3, gcc 3.4.4)
Fedora Linux	PowerPC	8.2.0	Build farm sponge (FC5, gcc 4.1.0)
Fedora Linux	x86	8.2.0	Build farm agouti (FC5, gcc 4.1.1); thrush (FC1, gcc 3.3.2)
FreeBSD	AMD64	8.2.0	Build farm platypus (6, gcc 3.4.4); dove (6.1, gcc 3.4.4); ermine (6.1, gcc 3.4.4)
FreeBSD	x86	8.2.0	Build farm minnow (6.1, gcc 3.4.4); echidna (6, gcc 3.4.2); herring (6, Intel cc 7.1)
Gentoo Linux	AMD64	8.1.0	Build farm caribou (2.6.9, gcc 3.3.5)
Gentoo Linux	IA64	8.2.0	Build farm stoat (2.6, gcc 3.3)
Gentoo Linux	PowerPC 64	8.2.0	Build farm cobra (1.4.16, gcc 3.4.3)
Gentoo Linux	x86	8.2.0	Build farm mongoose (1.6.14, icc 9.0.032)
HP-UX	IA64	8.2.0	Tom Lane (tgl@sss.pgh.pa.us), 2006-10-23 11.23, gcc and cc; see 'doc/FAQ_HPUX'
HP-UX	PA-RISC	8.2.0	Tom Lane (tgl@sss.pgh.pa.us), 2006-10-23 10.20 and 11.23, gcc and cc; see 'doc/FAQ_HPUX'
IRIX	MIPS	8.1.0	Kenneth Marshall (ktm@is.rice.edu), 2005-11-04 6.5, cc only
Kubuntu Linux	AMD64	8.2.0	Build farm rosella (5.10 "Breezy", gcc 4.0)
Mac OS X	PowerPC	8.2.0	Build farm tuna (10.4.2, gcc 4.0)
Mac OS X	x86	8.2.0	Build farm jackal (10.4.8, gcc 4.0.1)
Mandriva Linux	x86	8.2.0	Build farm gopher (Mandriva 2006, gcc 4.0.1)
NetBSD	m68k	8.2.0	Build farm osprey (2.0, gcc 3.3.3)
NetBSD	x86	8.2.0	Build farm gazelle (3.0, gcc 3.3.3); canary (1.6, gcc 2.95.3)
OpenBSD	AMD64	8.2.0	Build farm zebra (4.0, gcc 3.3.5)
OpenBSD	Sparc	8.0.0	Chris Mair (list@1006.org), 2005-01-10 3.3
OpenBSD	Sparc64	8.2.0	Build farm spoonbill (3.9, gcc 3.3.5)
OpenBSD	x86	8.2.0	Build farm emu (4.0, gcc 3.3.5); guppy (3.8, gcc 3.3.5) minor ecpg test failure on 3.8
Red Hat Linux	AMD64	8.1.0	Tom Lane (tgl@sss.pgh.pa.us), 2005-10-23 RHEL 4

Red Hat Linux	IA64	8.1.0	Tom Lane (tgl@sss.pgh.pa.us), 2005-10-23 RHEL 4
Red Hat Linux	PowerPC	8.1.0	Tom Lane (tgl@sss.pgh.pa.us), 2005-10-23 RHEL 4
Red Hat Linux	PowerPC 64	8.1.0	Tom Lane (tgl@sss.pgh.pa.us), 2005-10-23 RHEL 4
Red Hat Linux	S/390	8.1.0	Tom Lane (tgl@sss.pgh.pa.us), 2005-10-23 RHEL 4
Red Hat Linux	S/390x	8.1.0	Tom Lane (tgl@sss.pgh.pa.us), 2005-10-23 RHEL 4
Red Hat Linux	x86	8.1.0	Tom Lane (tgl@sss.pgh.pa.us), 2005-10-23 RHEL 4
Slackware Linux	x86	8.1.0	Sergey Koposov (math@sai.msu.ru), 2005-10-24 10.0
Solaris	Sparc	8.2.0	Build farm hyena (Solaris 10, gcc 3.4.3) see 'doc/FAQ_Solaris'
Solaris	x86	8.2.0	Build farm dragonfly (Solaris 9, gcc 3.2.3); kudu (Solaris 9, cc 5.3) see 'doc/FAQ_Solaris'
SUSE Linux	AMD64	8.1.0	Josh Berkus (josh@agliodbs.com), 2005-10-23 SLES 9.3
SUSE Linux	IA64	8.0.0	Reinhard Max (max@suse.de), 2005-01-03 SLES 9
SUSE Linux	PowerPC	8.0.0	Reinhard Max (max@suse.de), 2005-01-03 SLES 9
SUSE Linux	PowerPC 64	8.0.0	Reinhard Max (max@suse.de), 2005-01-03 SLES 9
SUSE Linux	S/390	8.0.0	Reinhard Max (max@suse.de), 2005-01-03 SLES 9
SUSE Linux	S/390x	8.0.0	Reinhard Max (max@suse.de), 2005-01-03 SLES 9
SUSE Linux	x86	8.0.0	Reinhard Max (max@suse.de), 2005-01-03 9.0, 9.1, 9.2, SLES 9

Tru64 UNIX	Alpha	8.1.0	Honda Shigehiro (fwif0083@mb.infoweb.ne.jp), 2005-11-01 5.0, cc 6.1-011
Ubuntu Linux	x86	8.2.0	Build farm caracara (6.06, gcc 4.0.3)
UnixWare	x86	8.2.0	Build farm warthog (7.1.4, cc 4.2) see 'doc/FAQ_SCO'
Windows	x86	8.2.0	Build farm yak (XP SP2, gcc 3.4.2); bandicoot (Windows 2000 Pro, gcc 3.4.2); snake (Windows Server 2003 SP1, gcc 3.4.2); trout (Windows Server 2000 SP4, gcc 3.4.2) see 'doc/FAQ_MINGW'
Windows with Cygwin	x86	8.2.0	Build farm eel (W2K Server SP4, gcc 3.4.4) see 'doc/FAQ_CYGWIN'
Yellow Dog Linux	PowerPC	8.1.0	Build farm carp (4.0, gcc 3.3.3)

Unsupported Platforms:.   The following platforms used to work but have not been tested recently. We include these here to let you know that these platforms *could* be supported if given some attention.

OS	PROCESSOR	VERSION	NOTES
Debian GNU/Linux	S/390	7.4	Noël Köthe (noel@debian.org), 2003-10-25
FreeBSD	Alpha	7.4	Peter Eisentraut (peter_e@gmx.net), 2003-10-25 4.8
Linux	PlayStation 2	8.0.0	Chris Mair (list@1006.org), 2005-01-09 requires --disable-spinlocks (works, but very slow)
NetBSD	Alpha	7.2	Thomas Thai (tom@minnesota.com), 2001-11-20 1.5W
NetBSD	arm32	7.4	Patrick Welche (prlw1@newn.cam.ac.uk), 2003-11-12 1.6ZE/acorn32
NetBSD	MIPS	7.2.1	Warwick Hunter (whunter@agile.tv), 2002-06-13 1.5.3
NetBSD	PowerPC	7.2	Bill Studenmund (wrstuden@netbsd.org), 2001-11-28 1.5
NetBSD	Sparc	7.4.1	Peter Eisentraut (peter_e@gmx.net), 2003-11-26 1.6.1, 32-bit

NetBSD	VAX	7.1	Tom I. Helbekkmo (tih@kpnQwest.no), 2001-03-30 1.5
SCO OpenServer	x86	7.3.1	Shibashish Satpathy (shib@postmark.net), 2002-12-11 5.0.4, gcc; see also 'doc/FAQ_SCO'
SunOS 4	Sparc	7.2	Tatsuo Ishii (t-ishii@sra.co.jp), 2001-12-04

2 Client-Only Installation on Windows

Although a complete PostgreSQL installation for Windows can only be built using MinGW or Cygwin, the C client library (libpq) and the interactive terminal (psql) can be compiled using other Windows tool sets. Makefiles are included in the source distribution for Microsoft Visual C++ and Borland C++. It should be possible to compile the libraries manually for other configurations.

> **Tip:** Using MinGW or Cygwin is preferred. If using one of those tool sets, see Chapter 1 *Installation Instructions*, page 5.

To build everything that you can on Windows using Microsoft Visual C++, change into the 'src' directory and type the command

```
nmake /f win32.mak
```

This assumes that you have Visual C++ in your path.

To build everything using Borland C++, change into the 'src' directory and type the command

```
make -N -DCFG=Release /f bcc32.mak
```

The following files will be built:

'interfaces\libpq\Release\libpq.dll'
> The dynamically linkable frontend library

'interfaces\libpq\Release\libpqdll.lib'
> Import library to link your programs to 'libpq.dll'

'interfaces\libpq\Release\libpq.lib'
> Static version of the frontend library

'bin\pg_config\Release\pg_config.exe'
'bin\psql\Release\psql.exe'
'bin\pg_dump\Release\pg_dump.exe'
'bin\pg_dump\Release\pg_dumpall.exe'
'bin\pg_dump\Release\pg_restore.exe'
'bin\scripts\Release\clusterdb.exe'
'bin\scripts\Release\createdb.exe'
'bin\scripts\Release\createuser.exe'
'bin\scripts\Release\createlang.exe'
'bin\scripts\Release\dropdb.exe'
'bin\scripts\Release\dropuser.exe'
'bin\scripts\Release\droplang.exe'
'bin\scripts\Release\vacuumdb.exe'
'bin\scripts\Release\reindexdb.exe'
> The PostgreSQL client applications and utilities.

Normally you do not need to install any of the client files. You should place the 'libpq.dll' file in the same directory as your applications .EXE-file. Only if this is for some reason not possible should you install it in the 'WINNT\SYSTEM32' directory (or in 'WINDOWS\SYSTEM' on a Windows 95/98/ME system). If this file is installed using a setup program, it should be installed with version checking using the VERSIONINFO resource included in the file, to ensure that a newer version of the library is not overwritten.

If you plan to do development using libpq on this machine, you will have to add the 'src\include' and 'src\interfaces\libpq' subdirectories of the source tree to the include path in your compiler's settings.

To use the library, you must add the 'libpqdll.lib' file to your project. (In Visual C++, just right-click on the project and choose to add it.)

3 Operating System Environment

This chapter discusses how to set up and run the database server and its interactions with the operating system.

3.1 The PostgreSQL User Account

As with any other server daemon that is accessible to the outside world, it is advisable to run PostgreSQL under a separate user account. This user account should only own the data that is managed by the server, and should not be shared with other daemons. (For example, using the user nobody is a bad idea.) It is not advisable to install executables owned by this user because compromised systems could then modify their own binaries.

To add a Unix user account to your system, look for a command useradd or adduser. The user name postgres is often used, and is assumed throughout this book, but you can use another name if you like.

3.2 Creating a Database Cluster

Before you can do anything, you must initialize a database storage area on disk. We call this a *database cluster*. (SQL uses the term catalog cluster.) A database cluster is a collection of databases that is managed by a single instance of a running database server. After initialization, a database cluster will contain a database named postgres, which is meant as a default database for use by utilities, users and third party applications. The database server itself does not require the postgres database to exist, but many external utility programs assume it exists. Another database created within each cluster during initialization is called template1. As the name suggests, this will be used as a template for subsequently created databases; it should not be used for actual work. (See Chapter 6 *Managing Databases*, page 93 for information about creating new databases within a cluster.)

In file system terms, a database cluster will be a single directory under which all data will be stored. We call this the *data directory* or *data area*. It is completely up to you where you choose to store your data. There is no default, although locations such as '/usr/local/pgsql/data' or '/var/lib/pgsql/data' are popular. To initialize a database cluster, use the command initdb, which is installed with PostgreSQL. The desired file system location of your database cluster is indicated by the -D option, for example

```
$ initdb -D /usr/local/pgsql/data
```

Note that you must execute this command while logged into the PostgreSQL user account, which is described in the previous section.

> **Tip:** As an alternative to the -D option, you can set the environment variable PGDATA.

initdb will attempt to create the directory you specify if it does not already exist. It is likely that it will not have the permission to do so (if you followed our advice and created an unprivileged account). In that case you should create the directory yourself (as root) and change the owner to be the PostgreSQL user. Here is how this might be done:

```
root# mkdir /usr/local/pgsql/data
root# chown postgres /usr/local/pgsql/data
root# su postgres
postgres$ initdb -D /usr/local/pgsql/data
```

initdb will refuse to run if the data directory looks like it has already been initialized.

Because the data directory contains all the data stored in the database, it is essential that it be secured from unauthorized access. initdb therefore revokes access permissions from everyone but the PostgreSQL user.

However, while the directory contents are secure, the default client authentication setup allows any local user to connect to the database and even become the database superuser. If you do not trust other local users, we recommend you use one of initdb's -W, --pwprompt or --pwfile options to assign a password to the database superuser. Also, specify -A md5 or -A password so that the default trust authentication mode is not used; or modify the generated 'pg_hba.conf' file after running initdb, *before* you start the server for the first time. (Other reasonable approaches include using ident authentication or file system permissions to restrict connections. See Chapter 7 *Client Authentication*, page 99 for more information.)

initdb also initializes the default locale for the database cluster. Normally, it will just take the locale settings in the environment and apply them to the initialized database. It is possible to specify a different locale for the database; more information about that can be found in Section 8.1 *Locale Support*, page 111. The sort order used within a particular database cluster is set by initdb and cannot be changed later, short of dumping all data, rerunning initdb, and reloading the data. There is also a performance impact for using locales other than C or POSIX. Therefore, it is important to make this choice correctly the first time.

initdb also sets the default character set encoding for the database cluster. Normally this should be chosen to match the locale setting. For details see Section 8.2 *Character Set Support*, page 114.

3.3 Starting the Database Server

Before anyone can access the database, you must start the database server. The database server program is called postgres. The postgres program must know where to find the data it is supposed to use. This is done with the -D option. Thus, the simplest way to start the server is:

```
$ postgres -D /usr/local/pgsql/data
```

which will leave the server running in the foreground. This must be done while logged into the PostgreSQL user account. Without -D, the server will try to use the data directory named by the environment variable PGDATA. If that variable is not provided either, it will fail.

Normally it is better to start postgres in the background. For this, use the usual shell syntax:

```
$ postgres -D /usr/local/pgsql/data >logfile 2>&1 &
```
It is important to store the server's stdout and stderr output somewhere, as
shown above. It will help for auditing purposes and to diagnose problems. (See
Section 9.3 *Log File Maintenance*, page 128 for a more thorough discussion of
log file handling.)

The postgres program also takes a number of other command-line options.
For more information, see the postgres reference page and Chapter 4 *Server
Configuration*, page 45 below.

This shell syntax can get tedious quickly. Therefore the wrapper program
pg_ctl is provided to simplify some tasks. For example:

```
pg_ctl start -l logfile
```
will start the server in the background and put the output into the named log
file. The -D option has the same meaning here as for postgres. pg_ctl is also
capable of stopping the server.

Normally, you will want to start the database server when the computer boots.
Autostart scripts are operating-system-specific. There are a few distributed
with PostgreSQL in the 'contrib/start-scripts' directory. Installing one will
require root privileges.

Different systems have different conventions for starting up daemons at boot
time. Many systems have a file '/etc/rc.local' or '/etc/rc.d/rc.local'. Others use 'rc.d' directories. Whatever you do, the server must be run by the PostgreSQL user account *and not by root* or any other user. Therefore you probably
should form your commands using su -c '...' postgres. For example:

```
su -c 'pg_ctl start -D /usr/local/pgsql/data -l serverlog'
  postgres
```
Here are a few more operating-system-specific suggestions. (In each case be
sure to use the proper installation directory and user name where we show
generic values.)

* For FreeBSD, look at the file 'contrib/start-scripts/freebsd' in the
  PostgreSQL source distribution.
* On OpenBSD, add the following lines to the file '/etc/rc.local':
  ```
  if [ -x /usr/local/pgsql/bin/pg_ctl -a -x
  /usr/local/pgsql/bin/postgres ]; then
      su - -c '/usr/local/pgsql/bin/pg_ctl start -l
  /var/postgresql/log -s' postgres
      echo -n ' postgresql'
  fi
  ```
* On Linux systems either add
  ```
  /usr/local/pgsql/bin/pg_ctl start -l logfile -D
  /usr/local/pgsql/data
  ```
  to '/etc/rc.d/rc.local' or look at the file 'contrib/start-scripts/linux'
  in the PostgreSQL source distribution.
* On NetBSD, either use the FreeBSD or Linux start scripts, depending on
  preference.

- On Solaris, create a file called '/etc/init.d/postgresql' that contains the following line:

  ```
  su - postgres -c "/usr/local/pgsql/bin/pg_ctl start -l
  logfile -D /usr/local/pgsql/data"
  ```

  Then, create a symbolic link to it in '/etc/rc3.d' as 'S99postgresql'.

While the server is running, its PID is stored in the file 'postmaster.pid' in the data directory. This is used to prevent multiple server instances from running in the same data directory and can also be used for shutting down the server.

3.3.1 Server Start-up Failures

There are several common reasons the server might fail to start. Check the server's log file, or start it by hand (without redirecting standard output or standard error) and see what error messages appear. Below we explain some of the most common error messages in more detail.

```
LOG:  could not bind IPv4 socket: Address already in use
HINT:  Is another postmaster already running on port 5432? If
 not, wait a few seconds and retry.
FATAL:  could not create TCP/IP listen socket
```

This usually means just what it suggests: you tried to start another server on the same port where one is already running. However, if the kernel error message is not Address already in use or some variant of that, there may be a different problem. For example, trying to start a server on a reserved port number may draw something like:

```
$ postgres -p 666
LOG:  could not bind IPv4 socket: Permission denied
HINT:  Is another postmaster already running on port 666? If
 not, wait a few seconds and retry.
FATAL:  could not create TCP/IP listen socket
```

A message like

```
FATAL:  could not create shared memory segment: Invalid argument
DETAIL:  Failed system call was shmget(key=5440001,
 size=4011376640, 03600).
```

probably means your kernel's limit on the size of shared memory is smaller than the work area PostgreSQL is trying to create (4011376640 bytes in this example). Or it could mean that you do not have System-V-style shared memory support configured into your kernel at all. As a temporary workaround, you can try starting the server with a smaller-than-normal number of buffers (shared_buffers). You will eventually want to reconfigure your kernel to increase the allowed shared memory size. You may also see this message when trying to start multiple servers on the same machine, if their total space requested exceeds the kernel limit.

An error like

```
FATAL:   could not create semaphores: No space left on device
DETAIL:   Failed system call was semget(5440126, 17, 03600).
```

does *not* mean you've run out of disk space. It means your kernel's limit on the number of System V semaphores is smaller than the number PostgreSQL wants to create. As above, you may be able to work around the problem by starting the server with a reduced number of allowed connections (max_connections), but you'll eventually want to increase the kernel limit.

If you get an "illegal system call" error, it is likely that shared memory or semaphores are not supported in your kernel at all. In that case your only option is to reconfigure the kernel to enable these features.

Details about configuring System V IPC facilities are given in Section 3.4.1 *Shared Memory and Semaphores*, page 32.

3.3.2 Client Connection Problems

Although the error conditions possible on the client side are quite varied and application-dependent, a few of them might be directly related to how the server was started up. Conditions other than those shown below should be documented with the respective client application.

```
psql: could not connect to server: Connection refused
Is the server running on host "server.joe.com" and accepting
TCP/IP connections on port 5432?
```

This is the generic "I couldn't find a server to talk to" failure. It looks like the above when TCP/IP communication is attempted. A common mistake is to forget to configure the server to allow TCP/IP connections.

Alternatively, you'll get this when attempting Unix-domain socket communication to a local server:

```
psql: could not connect to server: No such file or directory
Is the server running locally and accepting connections on
Unix domain socket "/tmp/.s.PGSQL.5432"?
```

The last line is useful in verifying that the client is trying to connect to the right place. If there is in fact no server running there, the kernel error message will typically be either Connection refused or No such file or directory, as illustrated. (It is important to realize that Connection refused in this context does *not* mean that the server got your connection request and rejected it. That case will produce a different message, as shown in Section 7.3 *Authentication problems*, page 110.) Other error messages such as Connection timed out may indicate more fundamental problems, like lack of network connectivity.

3.4 Managing Kernel Resources

A large PostgreSQL installation can quickly exhaust various operating system resource limits. (On some systems, the factory defaults are so low that you don't even need a really "large" installation.) If you have encountered this kind of problem, keep reading.

3.4.1 Shared Memory and Semaphores

Shared memory and semaphores are collectively referred to as "System V IPC" (together with message queues, which are not relevant for PostgreSQL). Almost all modern operating systems provide these features, but not all of them have them turned on or sufficiently sized by default, especially systems with BSD heritage. (For the Windows port, PostgreSQL provides its own replacement implementation of these facilities.)

The complete lack of these facilities is usually manifested by an Illegal system call error upon server start. In that case there's nothing left to do but to reconfigure your kernel. PostgreSQL won't work without them.

When PostgreSQL exceeds one of the various hard IPC limits, the server will refuse to start and should leave an instructive error message describing the problem encountered and what to do about it. (See also Section 3.3.1 *Server Start-up Failures*, page 30.) The relevant kernel parameters are named consistently across different systems; Table 3.1 gives an overview. The methods to set them, however, vary. Suggestions for some platforms are given below. Be warned that it is often necessary to reboot your machine, and possibly even recompile the kernel, to change these settings.

NAME	DESCRIPTION	REASONABLE VALUES
SHMMAX	Maximum size of shared memory segment (bytes)	at least several megabytes (see text)
SHMMIN	Minimum size of shared memory segment (bytes)	1
SHMALL	Total amount of shared memory available (bytes or pages)	if bytes, same as SHMMAX; if pages, ceil(SHMMAX/PAGE_SIZE)
SHMSEG	Maximum number of shared memory segments per process	only 1 segment is needed, but the default is much higher
SHMMNI	Maximum number of shared memory segments system-wide	like SHMSEG plus room for other applications
SEMMNI	Maximum number of semaphore identifiers (i.e., sets)	at least ceil(max_connections / 16)
SEMMNS	Maximum number of semaphores system-wide	ceil(max_connections / 16) * 17 plus room for other applications
SEMMSL	Maximum number of semaphores per set	at least 17
SEMMAP	Number of entries in semaphore map	see text
SEMVMX	Maximum value of semaphore	at least 1000 (The default is often 32767, don't change unless forced to)

Table 3.1: System V IPC parameters

The most important shared memory parameter is SHMMAX, the maximum size, in bytes, of a shared memory segment. If you get an error message from shmget like Invalid argument, it is likely that this limit has been exceeded. The size of the required shared memory segment varies depending on several PostgreSQL configuration parameters, as shown in Table 3.2. You can, as a temporary solution, lower some of those settings to avoid the failure. As a rough approximation, you can estimate the required segment size as 500 kB plus the variable amounts shown in the table. (Any error message you might get will include the exact size of the failed allocation request.) While it is possible to get PostgreSQL to run with SHMMAX as small as 1 MB, you need at least 4 MB for acceptable performance, and desirable settings are in the tens of megabytes.

Some systems also have a limit on the total amount of shared memory in the system (SHMALL). Make sure this is large enough for PostgreSQL plus any other applications that are using shared memory segments. (Caution: SHMALL is measured in pages rather than bytes on many systems.)

Less likely to cause problems is the minimum size for shared memory segments (SHMMIN), which should be at most approximately 500 kB for PostgreSQL (it is usually just 1). The maximum number of segments system-wide (SHMMNI) or per-process (SHMSEG) are unlikely to cause a problem unless your system has them set to zero.

PostgreSQL uses one semaphore per allowed connection (`max_connections`), in sets of 16. Each such set will also contain a 17th semaphore which contains a "magic number", to detect collision with semaphore sets used by other applications. The maximum number of semaphores in the system is set by SEMMNS, which consequently must be at least as high as `max_connections` plus one extra for each 16 allowed connections (see the formula in Table 3.1). The parameter SEMMNI determines the limit on the number of semaphore sets that can exist on the system at one time. Hence this parameter must be at least `ceil(max_connections / 16)`. Lowering the number of allowed connections is a temporary workaround for failures, which are usually confusingly worded "No space left on device", from the function `semget`.

In some cases it might also be necessary to increase SEMMAP to be at least on the order of SEMMNS. This parameter defines the size of the semaphore resource map, in which each contiguous block of available semaphores needs an entry. When a semaphore set is freed it is either added to an existing entry that is adjacent to the freed block or it is registered under a new map entry. If the map is full, the freed semaphores get lost (until reboot). Fragmentation of the semaphore space could over time lead to fewer available semaphores than there should be.

The SEMMSL parameter, which determines how many semaphores can be in a set, must be at least 17 for PostgreSQL.

Various other settings related to "semaphore undo", such as SEMMNU and SEMUME, are not of concern for PostgreSQL.

BSD/OS

Shared Memory. By default, only 4 MB of shared memory is supported. Keep in mind that shared memory is not pageable; it is locked in RAM. To increase the amount of shared memory supported by your system, add something like the following to your kernel configuration file:

```
options "SHMALL=8192"
options "SHMMAX=\(SHMALL*PAGE_SIZE\)"
```

SHMALL is measured in 4 kB pages, so a value of 1024 represents 4 MB of shared memory. Therefore the above increases the maximum shared memory area to 32 MB. For those running 4.3 or later, you will probably also need to increase KERNEL_VIRTUAL_MB above the default 248. Once all changes have been made, recompile the kernel, and reboot.

For those running 4.0 and earlier releases, use `bpatch` to find the `sysptsize` value in the current kernel. This is computed dynamically at boot time.

```
$ bpatch -r sysptsize
0x9 = 9
```

Next, add SYSPTSIZE as a hard-coded value in the kernel configuration file. Increase the value you found using `bpatch`. Add 1 for every additional 4 MB of shared memory you desire.

```
options "SYSPTSIZE=16"
```

sysptsize cannot be changed by sysctl.

Semaphores.   You will probably want to increase the number of semaphores as well; the default system total of 60 will only allow about 50 PostgreSQL connections. Set the values you want in your kernel configuration file, e.g.:

```
options "SEMMNI=40"
options "SEMMNS=240"
```

FreeBSD

The default settings are only suitable for small installations (for example, default SHMMAX is 32 MB). Changes can be made via the sysctl or loader interfaces. The following parameters can be set using sysctl:

```
$ sysctl -w kern.ipc.shmall=32768
$ sysctl -w kern.ipc.shmmax=134217728
$ sysctl -w kern.ipc.semmap=256
```

To have these settings persist over reboots, modify '/etc/sysctl.conf'.

The remaining semaphore settings are read-only as far as sysctl is concerned, but can be changed before boot using the loader prompt:

```
(loader) set kern.ipc.semmni=256
(loader) set kern.ipc.semmns=512
(loader) set kern.ipc.semmnu=256
```

Similarly these can be saved between reboots in '/boot/loader.conf'.

You might also want to configure your kernel to lock shared memory into RAM and prevent it from being paged out to swap. This can be accomplished using the sysctl setting kern.ipc.shm_use_phys.

If running in FreeBSD jails by enabling sysctl's security.jail.sysvipc_allowed, postmasters running in different jails should be run by different operating system users. This improves security because it prevents non-root users from interfering with shared memory or semaphores in a different jail, and it allows the PostgreSQL IPC cleanup code to function properly. (In FreeBSD 6.0 and later the IPC cleanup code doesn't properly detect processes in other jails, preventing the running of postmasters on the same port in different jails.)

FreeBSD versions before 4.0 work like NetBSD and OpenBSD (see below).

NetBSD
OpenBSD

The options SYSVSHM and SYSVSEM need to be enabled when the kernel is compiled. (They are by default.) The maximum size of shared memory is determined by the option SHMMAXPGS (in pages). The following shows an example of how to set the various parameters (OpenBSD uses option instead):

```
options          SYSVSHM
options          SHMMAXPGS=4096
options          SHMSEG=256

options          SYSVSEM
options          SEMMNI=256
options          SEMMNS=512
options          SEMMNU=256
options          SEMMAP=256
```

You might also want to configure your kernel to lock shared memory into RAM and prevent it from being paged out to swap. This can be accomplished using the sysctl setting kern.ipc.shm_use_phys.

HP-UX

The default settings tend to suffice for normal installations. On HP-UX 10, the factory default for SEMMNS is 128, which might be too low for larger database sites.

IPC parameters can be set in the System Administration Manager (SAM) under Kernel Configuration->Configurable Parameters. Hit Create A New Kernel when you're done.

Linux

The default settings are only suitable for small installations (the default max segment size is 32 MB). However the remaining defaults are quite generously sized, and usually do not require changes. The max segment size can be changed via the sysctl interface. For example, to allow 128 MB, and explicitly set the maximum total shared memory size to 2097152 pages (the default):

```
$ sysctl -w kernel.shmmax=134217728
$ sysctl -w kernel.shmall=2097152
```

In addition these settings can be saved between reboots in '/etc/sysctl.conf'.

Older distributions may not have the sysctl program, but equivalent changes can be made by manipulating the '/proc' file system:

```
$ echo 134217728 >/proc/sys/kernel/shmmax
$ echo 2097152 >/proc/sys/kernel/shmall
```

MacOS X

In OS X 10.2 and earlier, edit the file '/System/Library/StartupItems/ SystemTuning/SystemTuning' and change the values in the following commands:

```
sysctl -w kern.sysv.shmmax
sysctl -w kern.sysv.shmmin
sysctl -w kern.sysv.shmmni
sysctl -w kern.sysv.shmseg
sysctl -w kern.sysv.shmall
```

In OS X 10.3 and later, these commands have been moved to '/etc/rc' and must be edited there. Note that '/etc/rc' is usually overwritten by

OS X updates (such as 10.3.6 to 10.3.7) so you should expect to have to redo your editing after each update.

In OS X 10.3.9 and later, instead of editing '/etc/rc' you may create a file named '/etc/sysctl.conf', containing variable assignments such as

```
kern.sysv.shmmax=4194304
kern.sysv.shmmin=1
kern.sysv.shmmni=32
kern.sysv.shmseg=8
kern.sysv.shmall=1024
```

This method is better than editing '/etc/rc' because your changes will be preserved across system updates. Note that *all five* shared-memory parameters must be set in '/etc/sysctl.conf', else the values will be ignored.

Beware that recent releases of OS X ignore attempts to set SHMMAX to a value that isn't an exact multiple of 4096.

SHMALL is measured in 4 kB pages on this platform.

In all OS X versions, you'll need to reboot to make changes in the shared memory parameters take effect.

SCO OpenServer

In the default configuration, only 512 kB of shared memory per segment is allowed. To increase the setting, first change to the directory '/etc/conf/cf.d'. To display the current value of SHMMAX, run

```
./configure -y SHMMAX
```

To set a new value for SHMMAX, run

```
./configure SHMMAX=value
```

where *value* is the new value you want to use (in bytes). After setting SHMMAX, rebuild the kernel:

```
./link_unix
```

and reboot.

AIX

At least as of version 5.1, it should not be necessary to do any special configuration for such parameters as SHMMAX, as it appears this is configured to allow all memory to be used as shared memory. That is the sort of configuration commonly used for other databases such as DB/2.

It may, however, be necessary to modify the global ulimit information in '/etc/security/limits', as the default hard limits for file sizes (fsize) and numbers of files (nofiles) may be too low.

Solaris

At least in version 2.6, the default maximum size of a shared memory segments is too low for PostgreSQL. The relevant settings can be changed in '/etc/system', for example:

```
set shmsys:shminfo_shmmax=0x2000000
set shmsys:shminfo_shmmin=1
set shmsys:shminfo_shmmni=256
set shmsys:shminfo_shmseg=256

set semsys:seminfo_semmap=256
set semsys:seminfo_semmni=512
set semsys:seminfo_semmns=512
set semsys:seminfo_semmsl=32
```

You need to reboot for the changes to take effect.

UnixWare

On UnixWare 7, the maximum size for shared memory segments is only 512 kB in the default configuration. To display the current value of SHMMAX, run

```
/etc/conf/bin/idtune -g SHMMAX
```

which displays the current, default, minimum, and maximum values. To set a new value for SHMMAX, run

```
/etc/conf/bin/idtune SHMMAX value
```

where *value* is the new value you want to use (in bytes). After setting SHMMAX, rebuild the kernel:

```
/etc/conf/bin/idbuild -B
```

and reboot.

NAME	APPROXIMATE MULTIPLIER (BYTES PER INCREMENT)
max_connections	400 + 270 * max_locks_per_transaction
max_prepared_transactions	600 + 270 * max_locks_per_transaction
shared_buffers	8300 (assuming 8K BLCKSZ)
wal_buffers	8200 (assuming 8K XLOG_BLCKSZ)
max_fsm_relations	70
max_fsm_pages	6

Table 3.2: Configuration parameters affecting PostgreSQL's shared memory usage

3.4.2 Resource Limits

Unix-like operating systems enforce various kinds of resource limits that might interfere with the operation of your PostgreSQL server. Of particular importance are limits on the number of processes per user, the number of open files per process, and the amount of memory available to each process. Each of these have a "hard" and a "soft" limit. The soft limit is what actually counts but it can be changed by the user up to the hard limit. The hard limit can only be changed by the root user. The system call setrlimit is responsible for setting these parameters. The shell's built-in command ulimit (Bourne shells) or limit (csh) is used to control the resource limits from the command line. On BSD-derived systems the file '/etc/login.conf' controls the various resource limits set during login. See the operating system documentation for details. The relevant parameters are maxproc, openfiles, and datasize. For example:

```
default:\
    ...
            :datasize-cur=256M:\
            :maxproc-cur=256:\
            :openfiles-cur=256:\
    ...
```

(-cur is the soft limit. Append -max to set the hard limit.)

Kernels can also have system-wide limits on some resources.

* On Linux '/proc/sys/fs/file-max' determines the maximum number of open files that the kernel will support. It can be changed by writing a different number into the file or by adding an assignment in '/etc/sysctl.conf'. The maximum limit of files per process is fixed at the time the kernel is compiled; see '/usr/src/linux/Documentation/proc.txt' for more information.

The PostgreSQL server uses one process per connection so you should provide for at least as many processes as allowed connections, in addition to what you need for the rest of your system. This is usually not a problem but if you run several servers on one machine things might get tight.

The factory default limit on open files is often set to "socially friendly" values that allow many users to coexist on a machine without using an inappropriate fraction of the system resources. If you run many servers on a machine this is perhaps what you want, but on dedicated servers you may want to raise this limit.

On the other side of the coin, some systems allow individual processes to open large numbers of files; if more than a few processes do so then the system-wide limit can easily be exceeded. If you find this happening, and you do not want to alter the system-wide limit, you can set PostgreSQL's max_files_per_process configuration parameter to limit the consumption of open files.

3.4.3 Linux Memory Overcommit

In Linux 2.4 and later, the default virtual memory behavior is not optimal for PostgreSQL. Because of the way that the kernel implements memory over-commit, the kernel may terminate the PostgreSQL server (the master server process) if the memory demands of another process cause the system to run out of virtual memory.

If this happens, you will see a kernel message that looks like this (consult your system documentation and configuration on where to look for such a message):

```
Out of Memory: Killed process 12345 (postgres).
```

This indicates that the 'postgres' process has been terminated due to memory pressure. Although existing database connections will continue to function normally, no new connections will be accepted. To recover, PostgreSQL will need to be restarted.

One way to avoid this problem is to run PostgreSQL on a machine where you can be sure that other processes will not run the machine out of memory.

On Linux 2.6 and later, a better solution is to modify the kernel's behavior so that it will not "overcommit" memory. This is done by selecting strict overcommit mode via sysctl:

```
sysctl -w vm.overcommit_memory=2
```

or placing an equivalent entry in '/etc/sysctl.conf'. You may also wish to modify the related setting vm.overcommit_ratio. For details see the kernel documentation file 'Documentation/vm/overcommit-accounting'.

Some vendors' Linux 2.4 kernels are reported to have early versions of the 2.6 overcommit sysctl parameter. However, setting vm.overcommit_memory to 2 on a kernel that does not have the relevant code will make things worse not better. It is recommended that you inspect the actual kernel source code (see the function vm_enough_memory in the file 'mm/mmap.c') to verify what is supported in your copy before you try this in a 2.4 installation. The presence of the 'overcommit-accounting' documentation file should *not* be taken as evidence that the feature is there. If in any doubt, consult a kernel expert or your kernel vendor.

3.5 Shutting Down the Server

There are several ways to shut down the database server. You control the type of shutdown by sending different signals to the master postgres process.

SIGTERM
> After receiving SIGTERM, the server disallows new connections, but lets existing sessions end their work normally. It shuts down only after all of the sessions terminate normally. This is the *Smart Shutdown*.

SIGINT
> The server disallows new connections and sends all existing server processes SIGTERM, which will cause them to abort their current transactions and exit promptly. It then waits for the server processes to exit and finally shuts down. This is the *Fast Shutdown*.

SIGQUIT
> This is the *Immediate Shutdown*, which will cause the master postgres process to send a SIGQUIT to all child processes and exit immediately, without properly shutting itself down. The child processes likewise exit immediately upon receiving SIGQUIT. This will lead to recovery (by replaying the WAL log) upon next start-up. This is recommended only in emergencies.

The pg_ctl program provides a convenient interface for sending these signals to shut down the server.

Alternatively, you can send the signal directly using kill. The PID of the postgres process can be found using the ps program, or from the file 'postmaster.pid' in the data directory. For example, to do a fast shutdown:

```
$ kill -INT `head -1 /usr/local/pgsql/data/postmaster.pid`
```

Important: It is best not to use SIGKILL to shut down the server. Doing so will prevent the server from releasing shared memory and semaphores, which may then have to be done manually before a new server can be started. Furthermore, SIGKILL kills the postgres process without letting it relay the signal to its subprocesses, so it will be necessary to kill the individual subprocesses by hand as well.

3.6 Encryption Options

PostgreSQL offers encryption at several levels, and provides flexibility in protecting data from disclosure due to database server theft, unscrupulous administrators, and insecure networks. Encryption might also be required to secure sensitive data such as medical records or financial transactions.

Password Storage Encryption

By default, database user passwords are stored as MD5 hashes, so the administrator cannot determine the actual password assigned to the user. If MD5 encryption is used for client authentication, the unencrypted password is never even temporarily present on the server because the client MD5 encrypts it before being sent across the network.

Encryption For Specific Columns

The '/contrib' function library pgcrypto allows certain fields to be stored encrypted. This is useful if only some of the data is sensitive. The client supplies the decryption key and the data is decrypted on the server and then sent to the client.

The decrypted data and the decryption key are present on the server for a brief time while it is being decrypted and communicated between the client and server. This presents a brief moment where the data and keys can be intercepted by someone with complete access to the database server, such as the system administrator.

Data Partition Encryption

On Linux, encryption can be layered on top of a file system mount using a "loopback device". This allows an entire file system partition be encrypted on disk, and decrypted by the operating system. On FreeBSD, the equivalent facility is called GEOM Based Disk Encryption, or gbde.

This mechanism prevents unencrypted data from being read from the drives if the drives or the entire computer is stolen. This does not protect against attacks while the file system is mounted, because when mounted, the operating system provides an unencrypted view of the data. However, to mount the file system, you need some way for the encryption key to be passed to the operating system, and sometimes the key is stored somewhere on the host that mounts the disk.

Encrypting Passwords Across A Network

The MD5 authentication method double-encrypts the password on the client before sending it to the server. It first MD5 encrypts it based on the user name, and then encrypts it based on a random salt sent by the server when the database connection was made. It is this double-encrypted value that is sent over the network to the server. Double-encryption not only prevents the password from being discovered, it also prevents another connection from using the same encrypted password to connect to the database server at a later time.

Encrypting Data Across A Network

SSL connections encrypt all data sent across the network: the password, the queries, and the data returned. The 'pg_hba.conf' file allows administrators to specify which hosts can use non-encrypted connections (host) and which require SSL-encrypted connections (hostssl). Also, clients can specify that they connect to servers only via SSL. Stunnel or SSH can also be used to encrypt transmissions.

SSL Host Authentication

It is possible for both the client and server to provide SSL keys or certificates to each other. It takes some extra configuration on each side, but this provides stronger verification of identity than the mere use of passwords. It prevents a computer from pretending to be the server just long enough to read the password send by the client. It also helps prevent "man in the middle" attacks where a computer between the client and server pretends to be the server and reads and passes all data between the client and server.

Client-Side Encryption

If the system administrator cannot be trusted, it is necessary for the client to encrypt the data; this way, unencrypted data never appears on the database server. Data is encrypted on the client before being sent to the server, and database results have to be decrypted on the client before being used.

3.7 Secure TCP/IP Connections with SSL

PostgreSQL has native support for using SSL connections to encrypt client/server communications for increased security. This requires that OpenSSL is installed on both client and server systems and that support in PostgreSQL is enabled at build time (see Chapter 1 *Installation Instructions*, page 5).

With SSL support compiled in, the PostgreSQL server can be started with SSL enabled by setting the parameter ssl to on in 'postgresql.conf'. When starting in SSL mode, the server will look for the files 'server.key' and 'server.crt' in the data directory, which must contain the server private key and certificate, respectively. These files must be set up correctly before an SSL-enabled server can start. If the private key is protected with a passphrase, the server will prompt for the passphrase and will not start until it has been entered.

The server will listen for both standard and SSL connections on the same TCP port, and will negotiate with any connecting client on whether to use SSL. By default, this is at the client's option; see Section 7.1 *The pg_hba.conf file*, page 99 about how to set up the server to require use of SSL for some or all connections.

For details on how to create your server private key and certificate, refer to the OpenSSL documentation. A self-signed certificate can be used for testing, but a certificate signed by a certificate authority (CA) (either one of the global CAs or a local one) should be used in production so the client can verify the server's identity. To create a quick self-signed certificate, use the following OpenSSL command:

```
openssl req -new -text -out server.req
```

Fill out the information that openssl asks for. Make sure that you enter the local host name as "Common Name"; the challenge password can be left blank. The program will generate a key that is passphrase protected; it will not accept a passphrase that is less than four characters long. To remove the passphrase (as you must if you want automatic start-up of the server), run the commands

```
openssl rsa -in privkey.pem -out server.key
rm privkey.pem
```

Enter the old passphrase to unlock the existing key. Now do

```
openssl req -x509 -in server.req -text -key server.key -out
  server.crt
chmod og-rwx server.key
```

to turn the certificate into a self-signed certificate and to copy the key and certificate to where the server will look for them.

If verification of client certificates is required, place the certificates of the CA(s) you wish to check for in the file 'root.crt' in the data directory. When present, a client certificate will be requested from the client during SSL connection startup, and it must have been signed by one of the certificates present in 'root.crt'. (See Volume 2, Section 1.16 *SSL Support* for a description of how to set up client certificates.) Certificate Revocation List (CRL) entries are also checked if the file 'root.crl' exists.

When the 'root.crt' file is not present, client certificates will not be requested or checked. In this mode, SSL provides communication security but not authentication.

The files 'server.key', 'server.crt', 'root.crt', and 'root.crl' are only examined during server start; so you must restart the server to make changes in them take effect.

3.8 Secure TCP/IP Connections with SSH Tunnels

One can use SSH to encrypt the network connection between clients and a PostgreSQL server. Done properly, this provides an adequately secure network connection, even for non-SSL-capable clients.

First make sure that an SSH server is running properly on the same machine as the PostgreSQL server and that you can log in using ssh as some user. Then you can establish a secure tunnel with a command like this from the client machine:

```
ssh -L 3333:foo.com:5432 joe@foo.com
```

The first number in the -L argument, 3333, is the port number of your end of the tunnel; it can be chosen freely. The second number, 5432, is the remote end of the tunnel: the port number your server is using. The name or IP address between the port numbers is the host with the database server you are going to connect to. In order to connect to the database server using this tunnel, you connect to port 3333 on the local machine:

```
psql -h localhost -p 3333 postgres
```

To the database server it will then look as though you are really user joe@foo.com and it will use whatever authentication procedure was configured for connections from this user and host. Note that the server will not think the connection is SSL-encrypted, since in fact it is not encrypted between the SSH server and the PostgreSQL server. This should not pose any extra security risk as long as they are on the same machine.

In order for the tunnel setup to succeed you must be allowed to connect via ssh as joe@foo.com, just as if you had attempted to use ssh to set up a terminal session.

> **Tip:** Several other applications exist that can provide secure tunnels using a procedure similar in concept to the one just described.

4 Server Configuration

There are many configuration parameters that affect the behavior of the
database system. In the first section of this chapter, we describe how to set
configuration parameters. The subsequent sections discuss each parameter in
detail.

4.1 Setting Parameters

All parameter names are case-insensitive. Every parameter takes a value of
one of four types: Boolean, integer, floating point, or string. Boolean values
may be written as ON, OFF, TRUE, FALSE, YES, NO, 1, 0 (all case-insensitive) or
any unambiguous prefix of these.

Some settings specify a memory or time value. Each of these has an implicit unit, which is either kilobytes, blocks (typically eight kilobytes), milliseconds, seconds, or minutes. Default units can be queried by referencing pg_
settings.unit. For convenience, a different unit can also be specified explicitly. Valid memory units are kB (kilobytes), MB (megabytes), and GB (gigabytes);
valid time units are ms (milliseconds), s (seconds), min (minutes), h (hours), and
d (days). Note that the multiplier for memory units is 1024, not 1000.

One way to set these parameters is to edit the file 'postgresql.conf', which
is normally kept in the data directory. (initdb installs a default copy there.) An
example of what this file might look like is:

```
# This is a comment
log_connections = yes
log_destination = 'syslog'
search_path = '"$user", public'
shared_buffers = 128MB
```

One parameter is specified per line. The equal sign between name and value is
optional. Whitespace is insignificant and blank lines are ignored. Hash marks
(#) introduce comments anywhere. Parameter values that are not simple identifiers or numbers must be single-quoted. To embed a single quote in a parameter
value, write either two quotes (preferred) or backslash-quote.

In addition to parameter settings, the 'postgresql.conf' file can contain
include directives, which specify another file to read and process as if it were
inserted into the configuration file at this point. Include directives simply look
like

```
include 'filename'
```

If the file name is not an absolute path, it is taken as relative to the directory
containing the referencing configuration file. Inclusions can be nested.

The configuration file is reread whenever the main server process receives
a SIGHUP signal (which is most easily sent by means of pg_ctl reload). The
main server process also propagates this signal to all currently running server
processes so that existing sessions also get the new value. Alternatively, you can
send the signal to a single server process directly. Some parameters can only be

set at server start; any changes to their entries in the configuration file will be ignored until the server is restarted.

A second way to set these configuration parameters is to give them as a command-line option to the postgres command, such as:

    postgres -c log_connections=yes -c log_destination='syslog'

Command-line options override any conflicting settings in 'postgresql.conf'. Note that this means you won't be able to change the value on-the-fly by editing 'postgresql.conf', so while the command-line method may be convenient, it can cost you flexibility later.

Occasionally it is useful to give a command line option to one particular session only. The environment variable PGOPTIONS can be used for this purpose on the client side:

    env PGOPTIONS='-c geqo=off' psql

(This works for any libpq-based client application, not just psql.) Note that this won't work for parameters that are fixed when the server is started or that must be specified in 'postgresql.conf'.

Furthermore, it is possible to assign a set of parameter settings to a user or a database. Whenever a session is started, the default settings for the user and database involved are loaded. The commands ALTER USER and ALTER DATABASE, respectively, are used to configure these settings. Per-database settings override anything received from the postgres command-line or the configuration file, and in turn are overridden by per-user settings; both are overridden by per-session settings.

Some parameters can be changed in individual SQL sessions with the SET command, for example:

    SET ENABLE_SEQSCAN TO OFF;

If SET is allowed, it overrides all other sources of values for the parameter. Some parameters cannot be changed via SET: for example, if they control behavior that cannot be changed without restarting the entire PostgreSQL server. Also, some parameters can be modified via SET or ALTER by superusers, but not by ordinary users.

The SHOW command allows inspection of the current values of all parameters.

The virtual table pg_settings (described in pg_settings) also allows displaying and updating session run-time parameters. It is equivalent to SHOW and SET, but can be more convenient to use because it can be joined with other tables, or selected from using any desired selection condition.

4.2 File Locations

In addition to the 'postgresql.conf' file already mentioned, PostgreSQL uses two other manually-edited configuration files, which control client authentication (their use is discussed in Chapter 7 *Client Authentication*, page 99). By default, all three configuration files are stored in the database cluster's data directory. The parameters described in this section allow the configuration files to be placed elsewhere. (Doing so can ease administration. In particular it is often easier to ensure that the configuration files are properly backed-up when they are kept separate.)

data_directory (string)
>   Specifies the directory to use for data storage. This parameter can only be set at server start.

config_file (string)
>   Specifies the main server configuration file (customarily called 'postgresql.conf'). This parameter can only be set on the postgres command line.

hba_file (string)
>   Specifies the configuration file for host-based authentication (customarily called 'pg_hba.conf'). This parameter can only be set at server start.

ident_file (string)
>   Specifies the configuration file for ident authentication (customarily called 'pg_ident.conf'). This parameter can only be set at server start.

external_pid_file (string)
>   Specifies the name of an additional process-id (PID) file that the server should create for use by server administration programs. This parameter can only be set at server start.

In a default installation, none of the above parameters are set explicitly. Instead, the data directory is specified by the -D command-line option or the PGDATA environment variable, and the configuration files are all found within the data directory.

If you wish to keep the configuration files elsewhere than the data directory, the postgres -D command-line option or PGDATA environment variable must point to the directory containing the configuration files, and the data_directory parameter must be set in 'postgresql.conf' (or on the command line) to show where the data directory is actually located. Notice that data_directory overrides -D and PGDATA for the location of the data directory, but not for the location of the configuration files.

If you wish, you can specify the configuration file names and locations individually using the parameters config_file, hba_file and/or ident_file. config_file can only be specified on the postgres command line, but the others can be set within the main configuration file. If all three parameters plus data_directory are explicitly set, then it is not necessary to specify -D or PGDATA.

When setting any of these parameters, a relative path will be interpreted with respect to the directory in which postgres is started.

4.3 Connections and Authentication

4.3.1 Connection Settings

listen_addresses (string)

Specifies the TCP/IP address(es) on which the server is to listen for connections from client applications. The value takes the form of a comma-separated list of host names and/or numeric IP addresses. The special entry * corresponds to all available IP interfaces. If the list is empty, the server does not listen on any IP interface at all, in which case only Unix-domain sockets can be used to connect to it. The default value is localhost, which allows only local "loopback" connections to be made. This parameter can only be set at server start.

port (integer)

The TCP port the server listens on; 5432 by default. Note that the same port number is used for all IP addresses the server listens on. This parameter can only be set at server start.

max_connections (integer)

Determines the maximum number of concurrent connections to the database server. The default is typically 100 connections, but may be less if your kernel settings will not support it (as determined during initdb). This parameter can only be set at server start.

Increasing this parameter may cause PostgreSQL to request more System V shared memory or semaphores than your operating system's default configuration allows. See Section 3.4.1 *Shared Memory and Semaphores*, page 32 for information on how to adjust those parameters, if necessary.

superuser_reserved_connections (integer)

Determines the number of connection "slots" that are reserved for connections by PostgreSQL superusers. At most max_connections connections can ever be active simultaneously. Whenever the number of active concurrent connections is at least max_connections minus superuser_reserved_connections, new connections will be accepted only for superusers.

The default value is three connections. The value must be less than the value of max_connections. This parameter can only be set at server start.

unix_socket_directory (string)

Specifies the directory of the Unix-domain socket on which the server is to listen for connections from client applications. The default is normally '/tmp', but can be changed at build time. This parameter can only be set at server start.

unix_socket_group (string)

Sets the owning group of the Unix-domain socket. (The owning user of the socket is always the user that starts the server.) In combination with the parameter unix_socket_permissions this can be used as an additional access control mechanism for Unix-domain connections. By default this is the empty string, which selects the default group for the current user. This parameter can only be set at server start.

unix_socket_permissions (integer)

> Sets the access permissions of the Unix-domain socket. Unix-domain sockets use the usual Unix file system permission set. The parameter value is expected to be a numeric mode specification in the form accepted by the chmod and umask system calls. (To use the customary octal format the number must start with a 0 (zero).)
>
> The default permissions are 0777, meaning anyone can connect. Reasonable alternatives are 0770 (only user and group, see also unix_socket_group) and 0700 (only user). (Note that for a Unix-domain socket, only write permission matters and so there is no point in setting or revoking read or execute permissions.)
>
> This access control mechanism is independent of the one described in Chapter 7 *Client Authentication*, page 99.
>
> This parameter can only be set at server start.

bonjour_name (string)

> Specifies the Bonjour broadcast name. The computer name is used if this parameter is set to the empty string '' (which is the default). This parameter is ignored if the server was not compiled with Bonjour support. This parameter can only be set at server start.

tcp_keepalives_idle (integer)

> On systems that support the TCP_KEEPIDLE socket option, specifies the number of seconds between sending keepalives on an otherwise idle connection. A value of zero uses the system default. If TCP_KEEPIDLE is not supported, this parameter must be zero. This parameter is ignored for connections made via a Unix-domain socket.

tcp_keepalives_interval (integer)

> On systems that support the TCP_KEEPINTVL socket option, specifies how long, in seconds, to wait for a response to a keepalive before retransmitting. A value of zero uses the system default. If TCP_KEEPINTVL is not supported, this parameter must be zero. This parameter is ignored for connections made via a Unix-domain socket.

tcp_keepalives_count (integer)

> On systems that support the TCP_KEEPCNT socket option, specifies how many keepalives may be lost before the connection is considered dead. A value of zero uses the system default. If TCP_KEEPCNT is not supported, this parameter must be zero. This parameter is ignored for connections made via a Unix-domain socket.

4.3.2 Security and Authentication

authentication_timeout (integer)

Maximum time to complete client authentication, in seconds. If a would-be client has not completed the authentication protocol in this much time, the server breaks the connection. This prevents hung clients from occupying a connection indefinitely. The default is one minute (1m). This parameter can only be set in the 'postgresql.conf' file or on the server command line.

ssl (boolean)

Enables SSL connections. Please read Section 3.7 *Secure TCP/IP Connections with SSL*, page 42 before using this. The default is off. This parameter can only be set at server start.

password_encryption (boolean)

When a password is specified in CREATE USER or ALTER USER without writing either ENCRYPTED or UNENCRYPTED, this parameter determines whether the password is to be encrypted. The default is on (encrypt the password).

krb_server_keyfile (string)

Sets the location of the Kerberos server key file. See Section 7.2.3 *Kerberos authentication*, page 106 for details. This parameter can only be set at server start.

krb_srvname (string)

Sets the Kerberos service name. See Section 7.2.3 *Kerberos authentication*, page 106 for details. This parameter can only be set at server start.

krb_server_hostname (string)

Sets the host name part of the service principal. This, combined with krb_srvname, is used to generate the complete service principal, that is krb_srvname/krb_server_hostname@REALM. If not set, the default is the server host name. See Section 7.2.3 *Kerberos authentication*, page 106 for details. This parameter can only be set at server start.

krb_caseins_users (boolean)

Sets whether Kerberos user names should be treated case-insensitively. The default is off (case sensitive). This parameter can only be set at server start.

db_user_namespace (boolean)

This parameter enables per-database user names. It is off by default. This parameter can only be set in the 'postgresql.conf' file or on the server command line.

If this is on, you should create users as username@dbname. When username is passed by a connecting client, @ and the database name are appended to the user name and that database-specific user name is looked up by the server. Note that when you create users with names containing @ within the SQL environment, you will need to quote the user name.

With this parameter enabled, you can still create ordinary global users. Simply append @ when specifying the user name in the client. The @ will be stripped off before the user name is looked up by the server.

> **Note:** This feature is intended as a temporary measure until a complete solution is found. At that time, this option will be removed.

4.4 Resource Consumption

4.4.1 Memory

shared_buffers (integer)

Sets the amount of memory the database server uses for shared memory buffers. The default is typically 32 megabytes (32MB), but may be less if your kernel settings will not support it (as determined during initdb). This setting must be at least 128 kilobytes and at least 16 kilobytes times max_connections. (Non-default values of BLCKSZ change the minimum.) However, settings significantly higher than the minimum are usually needed for good performance. Several tens of megabytes are recommended for production installations. This parameter can only be set at server start.

Increasing this parameter may cause PostgreSQL to request more System V shared memory than your operating system's default configuration allows. See Section 3.4.1 *Shared Memory and Semaphores*, page 32 for information on how to adjust those parameters, if necessary.

temp_buffers (integer)

Sets the maximum number of temporary buffers used by each database session. These are session-local buffers used only for access to temporary tables. The default is eight megabytes (8MB). The setting can be changed within individual sessions, but only up until the first use of temporary tables within a session; subsequent attempts to change the value will have no effect on that session.

A session will allocate temporary buffers as needed up to the limit given by temp_buffers. The cost of setting a large value in sessions that do not actually need a lot of temporary buffers is only a buffer descriptor, or about 64 bytes, per increment in temp_buffers. However if a buffer is actually used an additional 8192 bytes will be consumed for it (or in general, BLCKSZ bytes).

max_prepared_transactions (integer)

Sets the maximum number of transactions that can be in the "prepared" state simultaneously (see PREPARE TRANSACTION (Volume 1)). Setting this parameter to zero disables the prepared-transaction feature. The default is five transactions. This parameter can only be set at server start.

If you are not using prepared transactions, this parameter may as well be set to zero. If you are using them, you will probably want max_prepared_ transactions to be at least as large as max_connections, to avoid unwanted failures at the prepare step.

Increasing this parameter may cause PostgreSQL to request more System V
shared memory than your operating system's default configuration allows.
See Section 3.4.1 *Shared Memory and Semaphores*, page 32 for information
on how to adjust those parameters, if necessary.

work_mem (integer)

Specifies the amount of memory to be used by internal sort operations
and hash tables before switching to temporary disk files. The value is
defaults to one megabyte (1MB). Note that for a complex query, several
sort or hash operations might be running in parallel; each one will be
allowed to use as much memory as this value specifies before it starts to
put data into temporary files. Also, several running sessions could be doing
such operations concurrently. So the total memory used could be many
times the value of work_mem; it is necessary to keep this fact in mind when
choosing the value. Sort operations are used for ORDER BY, DISTINCT, and
merge joins. Hash tables are used in hash joins, hash-based aggregation,
and hash-based processing of IN subqueries.

maintenance_work_mem (integer)

Specifies the maximum amount of memory to be used in maintenance operations, such as VACUUM, CREATE INDEX, and ALTER TABLE ADD FOREIGN KEY.
It defaults to 16 megabytes (16MB). Since only one of these operations can
be executed at a time by a database session, and an installation normally
doesn't have many of them running concurrently, it's safe to set this value
significantly larger than work_mem. Larger settings may improve performance for vacuuming and for restoring database dumps.

max_stack_depth (integer)

Specifies the maximum safe depth of the server's execution stack. The
ideal setting for this parameter is the actual stack size limit enforced by
the kernel (as set by ulimit -s or local equivalent), less a safety margin
of a megabyte or so. The safety margin is needed because the stack depth
is not checked in every routine in the server, but only in key potentially-
recursive routines such as expression evaluation. The default setting is two
megabytes (2MB), which is conservatively small and unlikely to risk crashes.
However, it may be too small to allow execution of complex functions. Only
superusers can change this setting.

Setting max_stack_depth higher than the actual kernel limit will mean that
a runaway recursive function can crash an individual backend process. On
platforms where PostgreSQL can determine the kernel limit, it will not let
you set this variable to an unsafe value. However, not all platforms provide
the information, so caution is recommended in selecting a value.

4.4.2 Free Space Map

These parameters control the size of the shared *free space map*, which tracks the locations of unused space in the database. An undersized free space map may cause the database to consume increasing amounts of disk space over time, because free space that is not in the map cannot be re-used; instead PostgreSQL will request more disk space from the operating system when it needs to store new data. The last few lines displayed by a database-wide VACUUM VERBOSE command can help in determining if the current settings are adequate. A NOTICE message is also printed during such an operation if the current settings are too low.

Increasing these parameters may cause PostgreSQL to request more System V shared memory than your operating system's default configuration allows. See Section 3.4.1 *Shared Memory and Semaphores*, page 32 for information on how to adjust those parameters, if necessary.

max_fsm_pages (integer)
> Sets the maximum number of disk pages for which free space will be tracked in the shared free-space map. Six bytes of shared memory are consumed for each page slot. This setting must be at least 16 * max_fsm_relations. The default is chosen by initdb depending on the amount of available memory, and can range from 20k to 200k pages. This parameter can only be set at server start.

max_fsm_relations (integer)
> Sets the maximum number of relations (tables and indexes) for which free space will be tracked in the shared free-space map. Roughly seventy bytes of shared memory are consumed for each slot. The default is one thousand relations. This parameter can only be set at server start.

4.4.3 Kernel Resource Usage

max_files_per_process (integer)
> Sets the maximum number of simultaneously open files allowed to each server subprocess. The default is one thousand files. If the kernel is enforcing a safe per-process limit, you don't need to worry about this setting. But on some platforms (notably, most BSD systems), the kernel will allow individual processes to open many more files than the system can really support when a large number of processes all try to open that many files. If you find yourself seeing "Too many open files" failures, try reducing this setting. This parameter can only be set at server start.

shared_preload_libraries (string)
> This variable specifies one or more shared libraries that are to be preloaded at server start. If more than one library is to be loaded, separate their names with commas. For example, '$libdir/mylib' would cause mylib.so (or on some platforms, mylib.sl) to be preloaded from the installation's standard library directory. This parameter can only be set at server start.

PostgreSQL procedural language libraries can be preloaded in this way, typically by using the syntax '$libdir/plXXX' where XXX is pgsql, perl, tcl, or python.

By preloading a shared library, the library startup time is avoided when the library is first used. However, the time to start each new server process may increase slightly, even if that process never uses the library. So this parameter is recommended only for libraries that will be used in most sessions.

> **Note:** On Windows hosts, preloading a library at server start will not reduce the time required to start each new server process; each server process will re-load all preload libraries. However, shared_preload_libraries is still useful on Windows hosts because some shared libraries may need to perform certain operations that only take place at postmaster start (for example, a shared library may need to reserve lightweight locks or shared memory and you can't do that after the postmaster has started).

If a specified library is not found, the server will fail to start.

Every PostgreSQL-supported library has a "magic block" that is checked to guarantee compatibility. For this reason, non-PostgreSQL libraries cannot be loaded in this way.

4.4.4 Cost-Based Vacuum Delay

During the execution of VACUUM and ANALYZE commands, the system maintains an internal counter that keeps track of the estimated cost of the various I/O operations that are performed. When the accumulated cost reaches a limit (specified by vacuum_cost_limit), the process performing the operation will sleep for a while (specified by vacuum_cost_delay). Then it will reset the counter and continue execution.

The intent of this feature is to allow administrators to reduce the I/O impact of these commands on concurrent database activity. There are many situations in which it is not very important that maintenance commands like VACUUM and ANALYZE finish quickly; however, it is usually very important that these commands do not significantly interfere with the ability of the system to perform other database operations. Cost-based vacuum delay provides a way for administrators to achieve this.

This feature is disabled by default. To enable it, set the vacuum_cost_delay variable to a nonzero value.

vacuum_cost_delay (integer)
> The length of time, in milliseconds, that the process will sleep when the cost limit has been exceeded. The default value is zero, which disables the cost-based vacuum delay feature. Positive values enable cost-based vacuuming. Note that on many systems, the effective resolution of sleep delays is 10 milliseconds; setting vacuum_cost_delay to a value that is not a multiple of 10 may have the same results as setting it to the next higher multiple of 10.

vacuum_cost_page_hit (integer)
> The estimated cost for vacuuming a buffer found in the shared buffer cache.
> It represents the cost to lock the buffer pool, lookup the shared hash table
> and scan the content of the page. The default value is one.

vacuum_cost_page_miss (integer)
> The estimated cost for vacuuming a buffer that has to be read from disk.
> This represents the effort to lock the buffer pool, lookup the shared hash
> table, read the desired block in from the disk and scan its content. The
> default value is 10.

vacuum_cost_page_dirty (integer)
> The estimated cost charged when vacuum modifies a block that was pre-
> viously clean. It represents the extra I/O required to flush the dirty block
> out to disk again. The default value is 20.

vacuum_cost_limit (integer)
> The accumulated cost that will cause the vacuuming process to sleep. The
> default value is 200.
>
> **Note:** There are certain operations that hold critical locks and should
> therefore complete as quickly as possible. Cost-based vacuum delays
> do not occur during such operations. Therefore it is possible that
> the cost accumulates far higher than the specified limit. To avoid
> uselessly long delays in such cases, the actual delay is calculated as
> vacuum_cost_delay * accumulated_balance / vacuum_cost_limit
> with a maximum of vacuum_cost_delay * 4.

4.4.5 Background Writer

Beginning in PostgreSQL 8.0, there is a separate server process called the
background writer, whose sole function is to issue writes of "dirty" shared
buffers. The intent is that server processes handling user queries should seldom
or never have to wait for a write to occur, because the background writer will
do it. This arrangement also reduces the performance penalty associated with
checkpoints. The background writer will continuously trickle out dirty pages
to disk, so that only a few pages will need to be forced out when checkpoint
time arrives, instead of the storm of dirty-buffer writes that formerly occurred
at each checkpoint. However there is a net overall increase in I/O load, because
where a repeatedly-dirtied page might before have been written only once per
checkpoint interval, the background writer might write it several times in the
same interval. In most situations a continuous low load is preferable to periodic
spikes, but the parameters discussed in this subsection can be used to tune the
behavior for local needs.

bgwriter_delay (integer)
> Specifies the delay between activity rounds for the background writer. In
> each round the writer issues writes for some number of dirty buffers (con-
> trollable by the following parameters). It then sleeps for bgwriter_delay
> milliseconds, and repeats. The default value is 200 milliseconds (200ms).
> Note that on many systems, the effective resolution of sleep delays is 10

milliseconds; setting `bgwriter_delay` to a value that is not a multiple of 10 may have the same results as setting it to the next higher multiple of 10. This parameter can only be set in the 'postgresql.conf' file or on the server command line.

`bgwriter_lru_percent (floating point)`

To reduce the probability that server processes will need to issue their own writes, the background writer tries to write buffers that are likely to be recycled soon. In each round, it examines up to `bgwriter_lru_percent` of the buffers that are nearest to being recycled, and writes any that are dirty. The default value is 1.0 (1% of the total number of shared buffers). This parameter can only be set in the 'postgresql.conf' file or on the server command line.

`bgwriter_lru_maxpages (integer)`

In each round, no more than this many buffers will be written as a result of scanning soon-to-be-recycled buffers. The default value is five buffers. This parameter can only be set in the 'postgresql.conf' file or on the server command line.

`bgwriter_all_percent (floating point)`

To reduce the amount of work that will be needed at checkpoint time, the background writer also does a circular scan through the entire buffer pool, writing buffers that are found to be dirty. In each round, it examines up to `bgwriter_all_percent` of the buffers for this purpose. The default value is 0.333 (0.333% of the total number of shared buffers). With the default `bgwriter_delay` setting, this will allow the entire shared buffer pool to be scanned about once per minute. This parameter can only be set in the 'postgresql.conf' file or on the server command line.

`bgwriter_all_maxpages (integer)`

In each round, no more than this many buffers will be written as a result of the scan of the entire buffer pool. (If this limit is reached, the scan stops, and resumes at the next buffer during the next round.) The default value is five buffers. This parameter can only be set in the 'postgresql.conf' file or on the server command line.

Smaller values of `bgwriter_all_percent` and `bgwriter_all_maxpages` reduce the extra I/O load caused by the background writer, but leave more work to be done at checkpoint time. To reduce load spikes at checkpoints, increase these two values. Similarly, smaller values of `bgwriter_lru_percent` and `bgwriter_lru_maxpages` reduce the extra I/O load caused by the background writer, but make it more likely that server processes will have to issue writes for themselves, delaying interactive queries. To disable background writing entirely, set both `maxpages` values and/or both `percent` values to zero.

4.5 Write Ahead Log

See also Section 14.3 *WAL Configuration*, page 173 for details on WAL tuning.

4.5.1 Settings

fsync (boolean)

If this parameter is on, the PostgreSQL server will try to make sure that updates are physically written to disk, by issuing fsync() system calls or various equivalent methods (see wal_sync_method (page 57)). This ensures that the database cluster can recover to a consistent state after an operating system or hardware crash.

However, using fsync results in a performance penalty: when a transaction is committed, PostgreSQL must wait for the operating system to flush the write-ahead log to disk. When fsync is disabled, the operating system is allowed to do its best in buffering, ordering, and delaying writes. This can result in significantly improved performance. However, if the system crashes, the results of the last few committed transactions may be lost in part or whole. In the worst case, unrecoverable data corruption may occur. (Crashes of the database software itself are *not* a risk factor here. Only an operating-system-level crash creates a risk of corruption.)

Due to the risks involved, there is no universally correct setting for fsync. Some administrators always disable fsync, while others only turn it off during initial bulk data loads, where there is a clear restart point if something goes wrong. Others always leave fsync enabled. The default is to enable fsync, for maximum reliability. If you trust your operating system, your hardware, and your utility company (or your battery backup), you can consider disabling fsync.

This parameter can only be set in the 'postgresql.conf' file or on the server command line. If you turn this parameter off, also consider turning off full_page_writes.

wal_sync_method (string)

Method used for forcing WAL updates out to disk. If fsync is off then this setting is irrelevant, since updates will not be forced out at all. Possible values are:

- open_datasync (write WAL files with open() option O_DSYNC)
- fdatasync (call fdatasync() at each commit)
- fsync_writethrough (call fsync() at each commit, forcing write-through of any disk write cache)
- fsync (call fsync() at each commit)
- open_sync (write WAL files with open() option O_SYNC)

Not all of these choices are available on all platforms. The default is the first method in the above list that is supported by the platform. The open_* options also use O_DIRECT if available. This parameter can only be set in the 'postgresql.conf' file or on the server command line.

`full_page_writes` (boolean)

When this parameter is on, the PostgreSQL server writes the entire content of each disk page to WAL during the first modification of that page after a checkpoint. This is needed because a page write that is in process during an operating system crash might be only partially completed, leading to an on-disk page that contains a mix of old and new data. The row-level change data normally stored in WAL will not be enough to completely restore such a page during post-crash recovery. Storing the full page image guarantees that the page can be correctly restored, but at a price in increasing the amount of data that must be written to WAL. (Because WAL replay always starts from a checkpoint, it is sufficient to do this during the first change of each page after a checkpoint. Therefore, one way to reduce the cost of full-page writes is to increase the checkpoint interval parameters.)

Turning this parameter off speeds normal operation, but might lead to a corrupt database after an operating system crash or power failure. The risks are similar to turning off fsync, though smaller. It may be safe to turn off this parameter if you have hardware (such as a battery-backed disk controller) or file-system software that reduces the risk of partial page writes to an acceptably low level (e.g., ReiserFS 4).

Turning off this parameter does not affect use of WAL archiving for point-in-time recovery (PITR) (see Section 10.3 *Continuous Archiving and Point-In-Time Recovery (PITR)*, page 135).

This parameter can only be set in the 'postgresql.conf' file or on the server command line. The default is on.

`wal_buffers` (integer)

The amount of memory used in shared memory for WAL data. The default is 64 kilobytes (64kB). The setting need only be large enough to hold the amount of WAL data generated by one typical transaction, since the data is written out to disk at every transaction commit. This parameter can only be set at server start.

Increasing this parameter may cause PostgreSQL to request more System V shared memory than your operating system's default configuration allows. See Section 3.4.1 *Shared Memory and Semaphores*, page 32 for information on how to adjust those parameters, if necessary.

`commit_delay` (integer)

Time delay between writing a commit record to the WAL buffer and flushing the buffer out to disk, in microseconds. A nonzero delay can allow multiple transactions to be committed with only one fsync() system call, if system load is high enough that additional transactions become ready to commit within the given interval. But the delay is just wasted if no other transactions become ready to commit. Therefore, the delay is only performed if at least commit_siblings other transactions are active at the instant that a server process has written its commit record. The default is zero (no delay).

commit_siblings (integer)

Minimum number of concurrent open transactions to require before performing the commit_delay delay. A larger value makes it more probable that at least one other transaction will become ready to commit during the delay interval. The default is five transactions.

4.5.2 Checkpoints

checkpoint_segments (integer)

Maximum distance between automatic WAL checkpoints, in log file segments (each segment is normally 16 megabytes). The default is three segments. This parameter can only be set in the 'postgresql.conf' file or on the server command line.

checkpoint_timeout (integer)

Maximum time between automatic WAL checkpoints, in seconds. The default is five minutes (5min). This parameter can only be set in the 'postgresql.conf' file or on the server command line.

checkpoint_warning (integer)

Write a message to the server log if checkpoints caused by the filling of checkpoint segment files happen closer together than this many seconds (which suggests that checkpoint_segments ought to be raised). The default is 30 seconds (30s). Zero disables the warning. This parameter can only be set in the 'postgresql.conf' file or on the server command line.

4.5.3 Archiving

archive_command (string)

The shell command to execute to archive a completed segment of the WAL file series. If this is an empty string (the default), WAL archiving is disabled. Any %p in the string is replaced by the path name of the file to archive, and any %f is replaced by the file name only. (The path name is relative to the working directory of the server, i.e., the cluster's data directory.) Use %% to embed an actual % character in the command. For more information see Section 10.3.1 *Setting up WAL archiving*, page 136. This parameter can only be set in the 'postgresql.conf' file or on the server command line.

It is important for the command to return a zero exit status if and only if it succeeds. Examples:

```
archive_command = 'cp "%p" /mnt/server/archivedir/"%f"'
archive_command = 'copy "%p" /mnt/server/archivedir/"%f"'
    # Windows
```

archive_timeout (integer)

The archive_command is only invoked on completed WAL segments. Hence, if your server generates little WAL traffic (or has slack periods where it does so), there could be a long delay between the completion of a transaction and its safe recording in archive storage. To put a limit on

how old unarchived data can be, you can set `archive_timeout` to force
the server to switch to a new WAL segment file periodically. When this
parameter is greater than zero, the server will switch to a new segment file
whenever this many seconds have elapsed since the last segment file switch.
Note that archived files that are closed early due to a forced switch are still
the same length as completely full files. Therefore, it is unwise to use a
very short `archive_timeout`—it will bloat your archive storage. `archive_`
`timeout` settings of a minute or so are usually reasonable. This parameter
can only be set in the 'postgresql.conf' file or on the server command
line.

4.6 Query Planning

4.6.1 Planner Method Configuration

These configuration parameters provide a crude method of influencing the
query plans chosen by the query optimizer. If the default plan chosen by the
optimizer for a particular query is not optimal, a temporary solution may be
found by using one of these configuration parameters to force the optimizer to
choose a different plan. Turning one of these settings off permanently is seldom
a good idea, however. Better ways to improve the quality of the plans chosen
by the optimizer include adjusting the Section 4.6.2 *Planner Cost Constants* ,
page 61, running `ANALYZE` more frequently, increasing the value of the `default_`
`statistics_target` configuration parameter, and increasing the amount of
statistics collected for specific columns using `ALTER TABLE SET STATISTICS`.

`enable_bitmapscan (boolean)`
> Enables or disables the query planner's use of bitmap-scan plan types. The
> default is on.

`enable_hashagg (boolean)`
> Enables or disables the query planner's use of hashed aggregation plan
> types. The default is on.

`enable_hashjoin (boolean)`
> Enables or disables the query planner's use of hash-join plan types. The
> default is on.

`enable_indexscan (boolean)`
> Enables or disables the query planner's use of index-scan plan types. The
> default is on.

`enable_mergejoin (boolean)`
> Enables or disables the query planner's use of merge-join plan types. The
> default is on.

`enable_nestloop (boolean)`
> Enables or disables the query planner's use of nested-loop join plans. It's
> not possible to suppress nested-loop joins entirely, but turning this vari-
> able off discourages the planner from using one if there are other methods
> available. The default is on.

enable_seqscan (boolean)

Enables or disables the query planner's use of sequential scan plan types. It's not possible to suppress sequential scans entirely, but turning this variable off discourages the planner from using one if there are other methods available. The default is on.

enable_sort (boolean)

Enables or disables the query planner's use of explicit sort steps. It's not possible to suppress explicit sorts entirely, but turning this variable off discourages the planner from using one if there are other methods available. The default is on.

enable_tidscan (boolean)

Enables or disables the query planner's use of TID scan plan types. The default is on.

4.6.2 Planner Cost Constants

The *cost* variables described in this section are measured on an arbitrary scale. Only their relative values matter, hence scaling them all up or down by the same factor will result in no change in the planner's choices. Traditionally, these variables have been referenced to sequential page fetches as the unit of cost; that is, seq_page_cost is conventionally set to 1.0 and the other cost variables are set with reference to that. But you can use a different scale if you prefer, such as actual execution times in milliseconds on a particular machine.

> **Note:** Unfortunately, there is no well-defined method for determining ideal values for the cost variables. They are best treated as averages over the entire mix of queries that a particular installation will get. This means that changing them on the basis of just a few experiments is very risky.

seq_page_cost (floating point)

Sets the planner's estimate of the cost of a disk page fetch that is part of a series of sequential fetches. The default is 1.0.

random_page_cost (floating point)

Sets the planner's estimate of the cost of a non-sequentially-fetched disk page. The default is 4.0. Reducing this value relative to seq_page_cost will cause the system to prefer index scans; raising it will make index scans look relatively more expensive. You can raise or lower both values together to change the importance of disk I/O costs relative to CPU costs, which are described by the following parameters.

> **Tip:** Although the system will let you set random_page_cost to less than seq_page_cost, it is not physically sensible to do so. However, setting them equal makes sense if the database is entirely cached in RAM, since in that case there is no penalty for touching pages out of sequence. Also, in a heavily-cached database you should lower both values relative to the CPU parameters, since the cost of fetching a page already in RAM is much smaller than it would normally be.

cpu_tuple_cost (floating point)
>   Sets the planner's estimate of the cost of processing each row during a
>   query. The default is 0.01.

cpu_index_tuple_cost (floating point)
>   Sets the planner's estimate of the cost of processing each index entry during
>   an index scan. The default is 0.005.

cpu_operator_cost (floating point)
>   Sets the planner's estimate of the cost of processing each operator or func-
>   tion executed during a query. The default is 0.0025.

effective_cache_size (integer)
>   Sets the planner's assumption about the effective size of the disk cache
>   that is available to a single query. This is factored into estimates of the
>   cost of using an index; a higher value makes it more likely index scans
>   will be used, a lower value makes it more likely sequential scans will be
>   used. When setting this parameter you should consider both PostgreSQL's
>   shared buffers and the portion of the kernel's disk cache that will be used
>   for PostgreSQL data files. Also, take into account the expected number
>   of concurrent queries on different tables, since they will have to share the
>   available space. This parameter has no effect on the size of shared memory
>   allocated by PostgreSQL, nor does it reserve kernel disk cache; it is used
>   only for estimation purposes. The default is 128 megabytes (128MB).

4.6.3 Genetic Query Optimizer

geqo (boolean)
>   Enables or disables genetic query optimization, which is an algorithm that
>   attempts to do query planning without exhaustive searching. This is on
>   by default. The geqo_threshold variable provides a more granular way to
>   disable GEQO for certain classes of queries.

geqo_threshold (integer)
>   Use genetic query optimization to plan queries with at least this many FROM
>   items involved. (Note that a FULL OUTER JOIN construct counts as only one
>   FROM item.) The default is 12. For simpler queries it is usually best to use
>   the deterministic, exhaustive planner, but for queries with many tables the
>   deterministic planner takes too long.

geqo_effort (integer)
>   Controls the trade off between planning time and query plan efficiency in
>   GEQO. This variable must be an integer in the range from 1 to 10. The
>   default value is five. Larger values increase the time spent doing query
>   planning, but also increase the likelihood that an efficient query plan will
>   be chosen.
>
>   geqo_effort doesn't actually do anything directly; it is only used to com-
>   pute the default values for the other variables that influence GEQO be-
>   havior (described below). If you prefer, you can set the other parameters
>   by hand instead.

geqo_pool_size (integer)

> Controls the pool size used by GEQO. The pool size is the number of
> individuals in the genetic population. It must be at least two, and useful
> values are typically 100 to 1000. If it is set to zero (the default setting)
> then a suitable default is chosen based on geqo_effort and the number of
> tables in the query.

geqo_generations (integer)

> Controls the number of generations used by GEQO. Generations specifies
> the number of iterations of the algorithm. It must be at least one, and
> useful values are in the same range as the pool size. If it is set to zero (the
> default setting) then a suitable default is chosen based on geqo_pool_size.

geqo_selection_bias (floating point)

> Controls the selection bias used by GEQO. The selection bias is the selec-
> tive pressure within the population. Values can be from 1.50 to 2.00; the
> latter is the default.

4.6.4 Other Planner Options

default_statistics_target (integer)

> Sets the default statistics target for table columns that have not had a
> column-specific target set via ALTER TABLE SET STATISTICS. Larger values
> increase the time needed to do ANALYZE, but may improve the quality of the
> planner's estimates. The default is 10. For more information on the use of
> statistics by the PostgreSQL query planner, refer to Volume 1, Section 11.2
> *Statistics Used by the Planner*.

constraint_exclusion (boolean)

> Enables or disables the query planner's use of table constraints to optimize
> queries. The default is off.
>
> When this parameter is on, the planner compares query conditions with
> table CHECK constraints, and omits scanning tables for which the conditions
> contradict the constraints. For example:
>
>  ```
>  CREATE TABLE parent(key integer, ...);
>  CREATE TABLE child1000(check (key between 1000 and 1999))
>   INHERITS(parent);
>  CREATE TABLE child2000(check (key between 2000 and 2999))
>   INHERITS(parent);
>  ...
>  SELECT * FROM parent WHERE key = 2400;
>  ```
>
> With constraint exclusion enabled, this SELECT will not scan child1000
> at all. This can improve performance when inheritance is used to build
> partitioned tables.
>
> Currently, constraint_exclusion is disabled by default because it risks
> incorrect results if query plans are cached—if a table constraint is changed
> or dropped, the previously generated plan might now be wrong, and there is
> no built-in mechanism to force re-planning. (This deficiency will probably
> be addressed in a future PostgreSQL release.) Another reason for keeping

it off is that the constraint checks are relatively expensive, and in many circumstances will yield no savings. It is recommended to turn this on only if you are actually using partitioned tables designed to take advantage of the feature.

Refer to Volume 1, Section 3.9 *Partitioning* for more information on using constraint exclusion and partitioning.

from_collapse_limit (integer)

The planner will merge sub-queries into upper queries if the resulting FROM list would have no more than this many items. Smaller values reduce planning time but may yield inferior query plans. The default is eight. It is usually wise to keep this less than geqo_threshold. For more information see Volume 1, Section 11.3 *Controlling the Planner with Explicit JOIN Clauses*.

join_collapse_limit (integer)

The planner will rewrite explicit JOIN constructs (except FULL JOINs) into lists of FROM items whenever a list of no more than this many items would result. Smaller values reduce planning time but may yield inferior query plans.

By default, this variable is set the same as from_collapse_limit, which is appropriate for most uses. Setting it to 1 prevents any reordering of explicit JOINs. Thus, the explicit join order specified in the query will be the actual order in which the relations are joined. The query planner does not always choose the optimal join order; advanced users may elect to temporarily set this variable to 1, and then specify the join order they desire explicitly. For more information see Volume 1, Section 11.3 *Controlling the Planner with Explicit JOIN Clauses*.

4.7 Error Reporting and Logging

4.7.1 Where To Log

log_destination (string)

PostgreSQL supports several methods for logging server messages, including stderr and syslog. On Windows, eventlog is also supported. Set this parameter to a list of desired log destinations separated by commas. The default is to log to stderr only. This parameter can only be set in the 'postgresql.conf' file or on the server command line.

redirect_stderr (boolean)

This parameter allows messages sent to stderr to be captured and redirected into log files. This method, in combination with logging to stderr, is often more useful than logging to syslog, since some types of messages may not appear in syslog output (a common example is dynamic-linker failure messages). This parameter can only be set at server start.

log_directory (string)

　　When redirect_stderr is enabled, this parameter determines the directory in which log files will be created. It may be specified as an absolute path, or relative to the cluster data directory. This parameter can only be set in the 'postgresql.conf' file or on the server command line.

log_filename (string)

　　When redirect_stderr is enabled, this parameter sets the file names of the created log files. The value is treated as a strftime pattern, so %-escapes can be used to specify time-varying file names. If no %-escapes are present, PostgreSQL will append the epoch of the new log file's open time. For example, if log_filename were server_log, then the chosen file name would be server_log.1093827753 for a log starting at Sun Aug 29 19:02:33 2004 MST. This parameter can only be set in the 'postgresql.conf' file or on the server command line.

log_rotation_age (integer)

　　When redirect_stderr is enabled, this parameter determines the maximum lifetime of an individual log file. After this many minutes have elapsed, a new log file will be created. Set to zero to disable time-based creation of new log files. This parameter can only be set in the 'postgresql.conf' file or on the server command line.

log_rotation_size (integer)

　　When redirect_stderr is enabled, this parameter determines the maximum size of an individual log file. After this many kilobytes have been emitted into a log file, a new log file will be created. Set to zero to disable size-based creation of new log files. This parameter can only be set in the 'postgresql.conf' file or on the server command line.

log_truncate_on_rotation (boolean)

　　When redirect_stderr is enabled, this parameter will cause PostgreSQL to truncate (overwrite), rather than append to, any existing log file of the same name. However, truncation will occur only when a new file is being opened due to time-based rotation, not during server startup or size-based rotation. When off, pre-existing files will be appended to in all cases. For example, using this setting in combination with a log_filename like postgresql-%H.log would result in generating twenty-four hourly log files and then cyclically overwriting them. This parameter can only be set in the 'postgresql.conf' file or on the server command line.

　　Example: To keep 7 days of logs, one log file per day named server_log.Mon, server_log.Tue, etc, and automatically overwrite last week's log with this week's log, set log_filename to server_log.%a, log_truncate_on_rotation to on, and log_rotation_age to 1440.

　　Example: To keep 24 hours of logs, one log file per hour, but also rotate sooner if the log file size exceeds 1GB, set log_filename to server_log.%H%M, log_truncate_on_rotation to on, log_rotation_age to 60, and log_rotation_size to 1000000. Including %M in log_filename allows any size-driven rotations that may occur to select a file name different from the hour's initial file name.

syslog_facility (string)

> When logging to syslog is enabled, this parameter determines the sys-log "facility" to be used. You may choose from LOCAL0, LOCAL1, LOCAL2, LOCAL3, LOCAL4, LOCAL5, LOCAL6, LOCAL7; the default is LOCAL0. See also the documentation of your system's syslog daemon. This parameter can only be set in the 'postgresql.conf' file or on the server command line.

syslog_ident (string)

> When logging to syslog is enabled, this parameter determines the program name used to identify PostgreSQL messages in syslog logs. The default is postgres. This parameter can only be set in the 'postgresql.conf' file or on the server command line.

4.7.2 When To Log

client_min_messages (string)

> Controls which message levels are sent to the client. Valid values are DEBUG5, DEBUG4, DEBUG3, DEBUG2, DEBUG1, LOG, NOTICE, WARNING, ERROR, FATAL, and PANIC. Each level includes all the levels that follow it. The later the level, the fewer messages are sent. The default is NOTICE. Note that LOG has a different rank here than in log_min_messages.

log_min_messages (string)

> Controls which message levels are written to the server log. Valid values are DEBUG5, DEBUG4, DEBUG3, DEBUG2, DEBUG1, INFO, NOTICE, WARNING, ERROR, LOG, FATAL, and PANIC. Each level includes all the levels that follow it. The later the level, the fewer messages are sent to the log. The default is NOTICE. Note that LOG has a different rank here than in client_min_messages. Only superusers can change this setting.

log_error_verbosity (string)

> Controls the amount of detail written in the server log for each message that is logged. Valid values are TERSE, DEFAULT, and VERBOSE, each adding more fields to displayed messages. Only superusers can change this setting.

log_min_error_statement (string)

> Controls whether or not the SQL statement that causes an error condition will be recorded in the server log. The current SQL statement is included in the log entry for any message of the specified severity or higher. Valid values are DEBUG5, DEBUG4, DEBUG3, DEBUG2, DEBUG1, INFO, NOTICE, WARNING, ERROR, FATAL, and PANIC. The default is ERROR, which means statements causing errors, fatal errors, or panics will be logged. To effectively turn off logging of failing statements, set this parameter to PANIC. Only superusers can change this setting.

log_min_duration_statement (integer)

> Causes the duration of each completed statement to be logged if the state-ment ran for at least the specified number of milliseconds. Setting this to zero prints all statement durations. Minus-one (the default) disables logging statement durations. For example, if you set it to 250ms then all SQL statements that run 250ms or longer will be logged. Enabling this

parameter can be helpful in tracking down unoptimized queries in your applications. Only superusers can change this setting.

For clients using extended query protocol, durations of the Parse, Bind, and Execute steps are logged independently.

> **Note:** When using this option together with `log_statement`, the text of statements that are logged because of `log_statement` will not be repeated in the duration log message. If you are not using syslog, it is recommended that you log the PID or session ID using `log_line_prefix` so that you can link the statement message to the later duration message using the process ID or session ID.

`silent_mode (boolean)`

Runs the server silently. If this parameter is set, the server will automatically run in background and any controlling terminals are disassociated. The server's standard output and standard error are redirected to `/dev/null`, so any messages sent to them will be lost. Unless syslog logging is selected or `redirect_stderr` is enabled, using this parameter is discouraged because it makes it impossible to see error messages. This parameter can only be set at server start.

Here is a list of the various message severity levels used in these settings:

`DEBUG[1-5]`

Provides information for use by developers.

`INFO`

Provides information implicitly requested by the user, e.g., during `VACUUM VERBOSE`.

`NOTICE`

Provides information that may be helpful to users, e.g., truncation of long identifiers and the creation of indexes as part of primary keys.

`WARNING`

Provides warnings to the user, e.g., `COMMIT` outside a transaction block.

`ERROR`

Reports an error that caused the current command to abort.

`LOG`

Reports information of interest to administrators, e.g., checkpoint activity.

`FATAL`

Reports an error that caused the current session to abort.

`PANIC`

Reports an error that caused all sessions to abort.

4.7.3 What To Log

debug_print_parse (boolean)
debug_print_rewritten (boolean)
debug_print_plan (boolean)
debug_pretty_print (boolean)

These parameters enable various debugging output to be emitted. For each executed query, they print the resulting parse tree, the query rewriter output, or the execution plan. debug_pretty_print indents these displays to produce a more readable but much longer output format. client_min_messages or log_min_messages must be DEBUG1 or lower to actually send this output to the client or the server log, respectively. These parameters are off by default.

log_connections (boolean)

This outputs a line to the server log detailing each successful connection. This is off by default, although it is probably very useful. Some client programs, like psql, attempt to connect twice while determining if a password is required, so duplicate "connection received" messages do not necessarily indicate a problem. This parameter can only be set in the 'postgresql.conf' file or on the server command line.

log_disconnections (boolean)

This outputs a line in the server log similar to log_connections but at session termination, and includes the duration of the session. This is off by default. This parameter can only be set in the 'postgresql.conf' file or on the server command line.

log_duration (boolean)

Causes the duration of every completed statement to be logged. The default is off. Only superusers can change this setting.

For clients using extended query protocol, durations of the Parse, Bind, and Execute steps are logged independently.

> **Note:** The difference between setting this option and setting log_min_duration_statement to zero is that exceeding log_min_duration_statement forces the text of the query to be logged, but this option doesn't. Thus, if log_duration is on and log_min_duration_statement has a positive value, all durations are logged but the query text is included only for statements exceeding the threshold. This behavior can be useful for gathering statistics in high-load installations.

log_line_prefix (string)

This is a printf-style string that is output at the beginning of each log line. The default is an empty string. Each recognized escape is replaced as outlined below—anything else that looks like an escape is ignored. Other characters are copied straight to the log line. Some escapes are only recognized by session processes, and do not apply to background processes such as the main server process. Syslog produces its own time stamp and process ID information, so you probably do not want to use those escapes if you are using syslog. This parameter can only be set in the 'postgresql.conf' file or on the server command line.

ESCAPE	EFFECT	SESSION ONLY
%u	User name	yes
%d	Database name	yes
%r	Remote host name or IP address, and remote port	yes
%h	Remote host name or IP address	yes
%p	Process ID	no
%t	Time stamp (no milliseconds, no timezone on Windows)	no
%m	Time stamp with milliseconds	no
%i	Command tag: This is the command that generated the log line.	yes
%c	Session ID: A unique identifier for each session. It is 2 4-byte hexadecimal numbers (without leading zeros) separated by a dot. The numbers are the session start time and the process ID, so this can also be used as a space saving way of printing these items.	yes
%l	Number of the log line for each process, starting at 1	no
%s	Session start time stamp	yes
%x	Transaction ID	yes
%q	Does not produce any output, but tells non-session processes to stop at this point in the string. Ignored by session processes.	no
%%	Literal %	no

log_statement (string)

Controls which SQL statements are logged. Valid values are none, ddl, mod, and all. ddl logs all data definition statements, such as CREATE, ALTER, and DROP statements. mod logs all ddl statements, plus data-modifying statements such as INSERT, UPDATE, DELETE, TRUNCATE, and COPY FROM. PREPARE, EXECUTE, and EXPLAIN ANALYZE statements are also logged if their contained command is of an appropriate type. For clients using extended query protocol, logging occurs when an Execute message is received, and values of the Bind parameters are included (with any embedded single-quote marks doubled).

The default is none. Only superusers can change this setting.

Note: Statements that contain simple syntax errors are not logged even by the log_statement = all setting, because the log message is emitted only after basic parsing has been done to determine the statement type. In the case of extended query protocol, this setting likewise does not log statements that fail before the Execute phase (i.e., during parse analysis or planning). Set log_min_error_statement to ERROR (or lower) to log such statements.

`log_hostname (boolean)`

> By default, connection log messages only show the IP address of the connecting host. Turning on this parameter causes logging of the host name as well. Note that depending on your host name resolution setup this might impose a non-negligible performance penalty. This parameter can only be set in the 'postgresql.conf' file or on the server command line.

4.8 Run-Time Statistics

4.8.1 Query and Index Statistics Collector

These parameters control a server-wide statistics collection feature. When statistics collection is enabled, the data that is produced can be accessed via the pg_stat and pg_statio family of system views. Refer to Chapter 12 *Monitoring Database Activity*, page 155 for more information.

> Note: As of PostgreSQL 8.2, stats_command_string controls a separate data collection mechanism that can be turned on or off independently of whether the statistics-collection subprocess is running. The subprocess is only needed to support collection of block-level or row-level statistics.

`stats_command_string (boolean)`

> Enables the collection of information on the currently executing command of each session, along with the time at which that command began execution. This parameter is on by default. Note that even when enabled, this information is not visible to all users, only to superusers and the user owning the session being reported on; so it should not represent a security risk. Only superusers can change this setting.

`update_process_title (boolean)`

> Enables updating of the process title every time a new SQL command is received by the server. The process title is typically viewed by the ps command or in Windows using the Process Explorer. Only superusers can change this setting.

`stats_start_collector (boolean)`

> Controls whether the server should start the statistics-collection subprocess. This is on by default, but may be turned off if you know you have no interest in collecting statistics or running autovacuum. This parameter can only be set at server start, because the collection subprocess cannot be started or stopped on-the-fly. (However, the extent to which statistics are actually gathered can be changed while the server is running, so long as the subprocess exists.)

`stats_block_level (boolean)`

> Enables the collection of block-level statistics on database activity. This parameter is off by default. Only superusers can change this setting.

`stats_row_level` (boolean)

> Enables the collection of row-level statistics on database activity. This parameter is off by default. Only superusers can change this setting.

`stats_reset_on_server_start` (boolean)

> If on, collected block-level and row-level statistics are zeroed out whenever the server is restarted. If off, statistics are accumulated across server restarts. This parameter is off by default. This parameter can only be set at server start.

4.8.2 Statistics Monitoring

`log_statement_stats` (boolean)
`log_parser_stats` (boolean)
`log_planner_stats` (boolean)
`log_executor_stats` (boolean)

> For each query, write performance statistics of the respective module to the server log. This is a crude profiling instrument. `log_statement_stats` reports total statement statistics, while the others report per-module statistics. `log_statement_stats` cannot be enabled together with any of the per-module options. All of these options are disabled by default. Only superusers can change these settings.

4.9 Automatic Vacuuming

These settings control the behavior of the *autovacuum* feature. Refer to Section 9.1.4 *The auto-vacuum daemon*, page 126 for more information.

`autovacuum` (boolean)   track - counts

> Controls whether the server should run the autovacuum daemon. This is off by default. stats_start_collector and stats_row_level must also be turned on for autovacuum to work. This parameter can only be set in the 'postgresql.conf' file or on the server command line.

`autovacuum_naptime` (integer)

> Specifies the delay between activity rounds for the autovacuum daemon. In each round the daemon examines one database and issues `VACUUM` and `ANALYZE` commands as needed for tables in that database. The delay is measured in seconds, and the default is one minute (1m). This parameter can only be set in the 'postgresql.conf' file or on the server command line.

`autovacuum_vacuum_threshold` (integer)

> Specifies the minimum number of updated or deleted tuples needed to trigger a `VACUUM` in any one table. The default is 500 tuples. This parameter can only be set in the 'postgresql.conf' file or on the server command line. This setting can be overridden for individual tables by entries in `pg_autovacuum`.

autovacuum_analyze_threshold (integer)

Specifies the minimum number of inserted, updated or deleted tuples needed to trigger an ANALYZE in any one table. The default is 250 tuples. This parameter can only be set in the 'postgresql.conf' file or on the server command line. This setting can be overridden for individual tables by entries in pg_autovacuum.

autovacuum_vacuum_scale_factor (floating point)

Specifies a fraction of the table size to add to autovacuum_vacuum_threshold when deciding whether to trigger a VACUUM. The default is 0.2 (20% of table size). This parameter can only be set in the 'postgresql.conf' file or on the server command line. This setting can be overridden for individual tables by entries in pg_autovacuum.

autovacuum_analyze_scale_factor (floating point)

Specifies a fraction of the table size to add to autovacuum_analyze_threshold when deciding whether to trigger an ANALYZE. The default is 0.1 (10% of table size). This parameter can only be set in the 'postgresql.conf' file or on the server command line. This setting can be overridden for individual tables by entries in pg_autovacuum.

autovacuum_freeze_max_age (integer)

Specifies the maximum age (in transactions) that a table's pg_class.relfrozenxid field can attain before a VACUUM operation is forced to prevent transaction ID wraparound within the table. Note that the system will launch autovacuum processes to prevent wraparound even when autovacuum is otherwise disabled. The default is 200 million transactions. This parameter can only be set at server start, but the setting can be reduced for individual tables by entries in pg_autovacuum. For more information see Section 9.1.3 *Preventing transaction ID wraparound failures*, page 124.

autovacuum_vacuum_cost_delay (integer)

Specifies the cost delay value that will be used in automatic VACUUM operations. If -1 is specified (which is the default), the regular vacuum_cost_delay value will be used. This parameter can only be set in the 'postgresql.conf' file or on the server command line. This setting can be overridden for individual tables by entries in pg_autovacuum.

autovacuum_vacuum_cost_limit (integer)

Specifies the cost limit value that will be used in automatic VACUUM operations. If -1 is specified (which is the default), the regular vacuum_cost_limit value will be used. This parameter can only be set in the 'postgresql.conf' file or on the server command line. This setting can be overridden for individual tables by entries in pg_autovacuum.

4.10 Client Connection Defaults

4.10.1 Statement Behavior

search_path (string)

This variable specifies the order in which schemas are searched when an object (table, data type, function, etc.) is referenced by a simple name with no schema component. When there are objects of identical names in different schemas, the one found first in the search path is used. An object that is not in any of the schemas in the search path can only be referenced by specifying its containing schema with a qualified (dotted) name.

The value for search_path has to be a comma-separated list of schema names. If one of the list items is the special value $user, then the schema having the name returned by SESSION_USER is substituted, if there is such a schema. (If not, $user is ignored.)

The system catalog schema, pg_catalog, is always searched, whether it is mentioned in the path or not. If it is mentioned in the path then it will be searched in the specified order. If pg_catalog is not in the path then it will be searched *before* searching any of the path items.

Likewise, the current session's temporary-table schema, pg_temp_*nnn*, is always searched if it exists. It can be explicitly listed in the path by using the alias pg_temp. If it is not listed in the path then it is searched first (before even pg_catalog). However, the temporary schema is only searched for relation (table, view, sequence, etc) and data type names. It will never be searched for function or operator names.

When objects are created without specifying a particular target schema, they will be placed in the first schema listed in the search path. An error is reported if the search path is empty.

The default value for this parameter is '"$user", public' (where the second part will be ignored if there is no schema named public). This supports shared use of a database (where no users have private schemas, and all share use of public), private per-user schemas, and combinations of these. Other effects can be obtained by altering the default search path setting, either globally or per-user.

The current effective value of the search path can be examined via the SQL function current_schemas(). This is not quite the same as examining the value of search_path, since current_schemas() shows how the requests appearing in search_path were resolved.

For more information on schema handling, see Volume 1, Section 3.7 *Schemas*.

default_tablespace (string)

This variable specifies the default tablespace in which to create objects (tables and indexes) when a CREATE command does not explicitly specify a tablespace.

The value is either the name of a tablespace, or an empty string to specify using the default tablespace of the current database. If the value does not match the name of any existing tablespace, PostgreSQL will automatically use the default tablespace of the current database.

For more information on tablespaces, see Section 6.6 *Tablespaces*, page 97.

check_function_bodies (boolean)
This parameter is normally on. When set to off, it disables validation of the function body string during CREATE FUNCTION. Disabling validation is occasionally useful to avoid problems such as forward references when restoring function definitions from a dump.

default_transaction_isolation (string)
Each SQL transaction has an isolation level, which can be either "read un-committed", "read committed", "repeatable read", or "serializable". This parameter controls the default isolation level of each new transaction. The default is "read committed".

Consult Volume 1, Chapter 10 *Concurrency Control* and SET TRANSACTION for more information.

default_transaction_read_only (boolean)
A read-only SQL transaction cannot alter non-temporary tables. This parameter controls the default read-only status of each new transaction. The default is off (read/write).

Consult SET TRANSACTION for more information.

statement_timeout (integer)
Abort any statement that takes over the specified number of milliseconds, starting from the time the command arrives at the server from the client. If log_min_error_statement is set to ERROR or lower, the statement that timed out will also be logged. A value of zero (the default) turns off the limitation.

vacuum_freeze_min_age (integer)
Specifies the cutoff age (in transactions) that VACUUM should use to decide whether to replace transaction IDs with FrozenXID while scanning a table. The default is 100 million transactions. Although users can set this value anywhere from zero to one billion, VACUUM will silently limit the effective value to half the value of autovacuum_freeze_max_age, so that there is not an unreasonably short time between forced autovacuums. For more information see Section 9.1.3 *Preventing transaction ID wraparound failures*, page 124.

4.10.2 Locale and Formatting

DateStyle (string)

Sets the display format for date and time values, as well as the rules for interpreting ambiguous date input values. For historical reasons, this variable contains two independent components: the output format specification (ISO, Postgres, SQL, or German) and the input/output specification for year/month/day ordering (DMY, MDY, or YMD). These can be set separately or together. The keywords Euro and European are synonyms for DMY; the keywords US, NonEuro, and NonEuropean are synonyms for MDY. See Volume 1, Section 6.5 *Date/Time Types* for more information. The built-in default is ISO, MDY, but initdb will initialize the configuration file with a setting that corresponds to the behavior of the chosen lc_time locale.

timezone (string)

Sets the time zone for displaying and interpreting time stamps. The default is 'unknown', which means to use whatever the system environment specifies as the time zone. See Volume 1, Section 6.5 *Date/Time Types* for more information.

timezone_abbreviations (string)

Sets the collection of time zone abbreviations that will be accepted by the server for datetime input. The default is 'Default', which is a collection that works in most of the world; there are also 'Australia' and 'India', and other collections can be defined for a particular installation. See Volume 1, Appendix B *Date/Time Support* for more information.

extra_float_digits (integer)

This parameter adjusts the number of digits displayed for floating-point values, including float4, float8, and geometric data types. The parameter value is added to the standard number of digits (FLT_DIG or DBL_DIG as appropriate). The value can be set as high as 2, to include partially-significant digits; this is especially useful for dumping float data that needs to be restored exactly. Or it can be set negative to suppress unwanted digits.

client_encoding (string)

Sets the client-side encoding (character set). The default is to use the database encoding.

lc_messages (string)

Sets the language in which messages are displayed. Acceptable values are system-dependent; see Section 8.1 *Locale Support*, page 111 for more information. If this variable is set to the empty string (which is the default) then the value is inherited from the execution environment of the server in a system-dependent way.

On some systems, this locale category does not exist. Setting this variable will still work, but there will be no effect. Also, there is a chance that no translated messages for the desired language exist. In that case you will continue to see the English messages.

Only superusers can change this setting, because it affects the messages
sent to the server log as well as to the client.

lc_monetary (string)
    Sets the locale to use for formatting monetary amounts, for example with
    the to_char family of functions. Acceptable values are system-dependent;
    see Section 8.1 *Locale Support*, page 111 for more information. If this
    variable is set to the empty string (which is the default) then the value
    is inherited from the execution environment of the server in a system-
    dependent way.

lc_numeric (string)
    Sets the locale to use for formatting numbers, for example with the to_
    char family of functions. Acceptable values are system-dependent; see
    Section 8.1 *Locale Support*, page 111 for more information. If this variable
    is set to the empty string (which is the default) then the value is inherited
    from the execution environment of the server in a system-dependent way.

lc_time (string)
    Sets the locale to use for formatting date and time values. (Currently,
    this setting does nothing, but it may in the future.) Acceptable values
    are system-dependent; see Section 8.1 *Locale Support*, page 111 for more
    information. If this variable is set to the empty string (which is the default)
    then the value is inherited from the execution environment of the server in
    a system-dependent way.

4.10.3 Other Defaults

explain_pretty_print (boolean)
    Determines whether EXPLAIN VERBOSE uses the indented or non-indented
    format for displaying detailed query-tree dumps. The default is on.

dynamic_library_path (string)
    If a dynamically loadable module needs to be opened and the file name
    specified in the CREATE FUNCTION or LOAD command does not have a direc-
    tory component (i.e. the name does not contain a slash), the system will
    search this path for the required file.

    The value for dynamic_library_path has to be a list of absolute directory
    paths separated by colons (or semi-colons on Windows). If a list element
    starts with the special string $libdir, the compiled-in PostgreSQL package
    library directory is substituted for $libdir. This is where the modules
    provided by the standard PostgreSQL distribution are installed. (Use pg_
    config --pkglibdir to find out the name of this directory.) For example:

        dynamic_library_path = '/usr/local/lib/postgresql:/home/
        my_project/lib:$libdir'

    or, in a Windows environment:

```
dynamic_library_path = 'C:\tools\postgresql;
H:\my_project\lib;$libdir'
```

The default value for this parameter is '$libdir'. If the value is set to an empty string, the automatic path search is turned off.

This parameter can be changed at run time by superusers, but a setting done that way will only persist until the end of the client connection, so this method should be reserved for development purposes. The recommended way to set this parameter is in the 'postgresql.conf' configuration file.

gin_fuzzy_search_limit (integer)

Soft upper limit of the size of the set returned by GIN index. For more information see Volume 4, Section 10.4 *GIN tips and tricks*.

local_preload_libraries (string)

This variable specifies one or more shared libraries that are to be preloaded at connection start. If more than one library is to be loaded, separate their names with commas. This parameter cannot be changed after the start of a particular session.

Because this is not a superuser-only option, the libraries that can be loaded are restricted to those appearing in the 'plugins' subdirectory of the installation's standard library directory. (It is the database administrator's responsibility to ensure that only "safe" libraries are installed there.) Entries in local_preload_libraries can specify this directory explicitly, for example $libdir/plugins/mylib, or just specify the library name—mylib would have the same effect as $libdir/plugins/mylib.

There is no performance advantage to loading a library at session start rather than when it is first used. Rather, the intent of this feature is to allow debugging or performance-measurement libraries to be loaded into specific sessions without an explicit LOAD command being given. For example, debugging could be enabled for all sessions under a given user name by setting this parameter with ALTER USER SET.

If a specified library is not found, the connection attempt will fail.

Every PostgreSQL-supported library has a "magic block" that is checked to guarantee compatibility. For this reason, non-PostgreSQL libraries cannot be loaded in this way.

4.11 Lock Management

deadlock_timeout (integer)
>   This is the amount of time, in milliseconds, to wait on a lock before check-
>   ing to see if there is a deadlock condition. The check for deadlock is
>   relatively slow, so the server doesn't run it every time it waits for a lock.
>   We (optimistically?) assume that deadlocks are not common in production
>   applications and just wait on the lock for a while before starting the check
>   for a deadlock. Increasing this value reduces the amount of time wasted in
>   needless deadlock checks, but slows down reporting of real deadlock errors.
>   The default is one second (1s), which is probably about the smallest value
>   you would want in practice. On a heavily loaded server you might want
>   to raise it. Ideally the setting should exceed your typical transaction time,
>   so as to improve the odds that a lock will be released before the waiter
>   decides to check for deadlock.

max_locks_per_transaction (integer)
>   The shared lock table is created to track locks on max_locks_per_
>   transaction * (max_connections + max_prepared_transactions) objects
>   (e.g. tables); hence, no more than this many distinct objects can be locked
>   at any one time. This parameter controls the average number of object
>   locks allocated for each transaction; individual transactions can lock more
>   objects as long as the locks of all transactions fit in the lock table. This is
>   *not* the number of rows that can be locked; that value is unlimited. The
>   default, 64, has historically proven sufficient, but you might need to raise
>   this value if you have clients that touch many different tables in a single
>   transaction. This parameter can only be set at server start.
>
>   Increasing this parameter may cause PostgreSQL to request more System V
>   shared memory than your operating system's default configuration allows.
>   See Section 3.4.1 *Shared Memory and Semaphores*, page 32 for information
>   on how to adjust those parameters, if necessary.

4.12 Version and Platform Compatibility

4.12.1 Previous PostgreSQL Versions

add_missing_from (boolean)
>   When on, tables that are referenced by a query will be automatically added
>   to the FROM clause if not already present. This behavior does not comply
>   with the SQL standard and many people dislike it because it can mask
>   mistakes (such as referencing a table where you should have referenced its
>   alias). The default is off. This variable can be enabled for compatibility
>   with releases of PostgreSQL prior to 8.1, where this behavior was allowed
>   by default.
>
>   Note that even when this variable is enabled, a warning message will be
>   emitted for each implicit FROM entry referenced by a query. Users are
>   encouraged to update their applications to not rely on this behavior, by

adding all tables referenced by a query to the query's FROM clause (or its USING clause in the case of DELETE).

array_nulls (boolean)

This controls whether the array input parser recognizes unquoted NULL as specifying a null array element. By default, this is on, allowing array values containing null values to be entered. However, PostgreSQL versions before 8.2 did not support null values in arrays, and therefore would treat NULL as specifying a normal array element with the string value "NULL". For backwards compatibility with applications that require the old behavior, this variable can be turned off.

Note that it is possible to create array values containing null values even when this variable is off.

backslash_quote (string)

This controls whether a quote mark can be represented by \' in a string literal. The preferred, SQL-standard way to represent a quote mark is by doubling it ('') but PostgreSQL has historically also accepted \'. However, use of \' creates security risks because in some client character set encodings, there are multibyte characters in which the last byte is numerically equivalent to ASCII \. If client-side code does escaping incorrectly then a SQL-injection attack is possible. This risk can be prevented by making the server reject queries in which a quote mark appears to be escaped by a backslash. The allowed values of backslash_quote are on (allow \' always), off (reject always), and safe_encoding (allow only if client encoding does not allow ASCII \ within a multibyte character). safe_encoding is the default setting.

Note that in a standard-conforming string literal, \ just means \ anyway. This parameter affects the handling of non-standard-conforming literals, including escape string syntax (E'...').

default_with_oids (boolean)

This controls whether CREATE TABLE and CREATE TABLE AS include an OID column in newly-created tables, if neither WITH OIDS nor WITHOUT OIDS is specified. It also determines whether OIDs will be included in tables created by SELECT INTO. In PostgreSQL 8.1 default_with_oids is off by default; in prior versions of PostgreSQL, it was on by default.

The use of OIDs in user tables is considered deprecated, so most installations should leave this variable disabled. Applications that require OIDs for a particular table should specify WITH OIDS when creating the table. This variable can be enabled for compatibility with old applications that do not follow this behavior.

escape_string_warning (boolean)

When on, a warning is issued if a backslash (\) appears in an ordinary string literal ('...' syntax) and standard_conforming_strings is off. The default is on.

Applications that wish to use backslash as escape should be modified to use escape string syntax (E'...'), because the default behavior of ordinary

strings will change in a future release for SQL compatibility. This variable
can be enabled to help detect applications that will break.

regex_flavor (string)
    The regular expression "flavor" can be set to advanced, extended, or
    basic. The default is advanced. The extended setting may be useful for
    exact backwards compatibility with pre-7.4 releases of PostgreSQL. See
    Volume 1, Section 7.7.3.1 *Regular Expression Details* for details.

sql_inheritance (boolean)
    This controls the inheritance semantics. If turned off, subtables are not
    included by various commands by default; basically an implied ONLY key
    word. This was added for compatibility with releases prior to 7.1. See
    Volume 1, Section 3.8 *Inheritance* for more information.

standard_conforming_strings (boolean)
    This controls whether ordinary string literals ('...') treat backslashes
    literally, as specified in the SQL standard. The default is currently off,
    causing PostgreSQL to have its historical behavior of treating backslashes
    as escape characters. The default will change to on in a future release
    to improve compatibility with the standard. Applications may check this
    parameter to determine how string literals will be processed. The presence
    of this parameter can also be taken as an indication that the escape string
    syntax (E'...') is supported. Escape string syntax should be used if an
    application desires backslashes to be treated as escape characters.

4.12.2 Platform and Client Compatibility

transform_null_equals (boolean)
    When on, expressions of the form *expr* = NULL (or NULL = *expr*) are treated
    as *expr* IS NULL, that is, they return true if *expr* evaluates to the null value,
    and false otherwise. The correct SQL-spec-compliant behavior of *expr* =
    NULL is to always return null (unknown). Therefore this parameter defaults
    to off.

    However, filtered forms in Microsoft Access generate queries that appear to
    use *expr* = NULL to test for null values, so if you use that interface to access
    the database you might want to turn this option on. Since expressions
    of the form *expr* = NULL always return the null value (using the correct
    interpretation) they are not very useful and do not appear often in normal
    applications, so this option does little harm in practice. But new users
    are frequently confused about the semantics of expressions involving null
    values, so this option is not on by default.

    Note that this option only affects the exact form = NULL, not other com-
    parison operators or other expressions that are computationally equivalent
    to some expression involving the equals operator (such as IN). Thus, this
    option is not a general fix for bad programming.

    Refer to Volume 1, Section 7.2 *Comparison Operators* for related informa-
    tion.

4.13 Preset Options

The following "parameters" are read-only, and are determined when PostgreSQL is compiled or when it is installed. As such, they have been excluded
from the sample 'postgresql.conf' file. These options report various aspects
of PostgreSQL behavior that may be of interest to certain applications, particularly administrative front-ends.

block_size (integer)

> Reports the size of a disk block. It is determined by the value of BLCKSZ
> when building the server. The default value is 8192 bytes. The meaning
> of some configuration variables (such as shared_buffers) is influenced by
> block_size. See Section 4.4 *Resource Consumption*, page 51 for informa-
> tion.

integer_datetimes (boolean)

> Reports whether PostgreSQL was built with support for 64-bit-integer
> dates and times. It is set by configuring with --enable-integer-
> datetimes when building PostgreSQL. The default value is off.

lc_collate (string)

> Reports the locale in which sorting of textual data is done. See Section 8.1
> *Locale Support*, page 111 for more information. The value is determined
> when the database cluster is initialized.

lc_ctype (string)

> Reports the locale that determines character classifications. See Section 8.1
> *Locale Support*, page 111 for more information. The value is determined
> when the database cluster is initialized. Ordinarily this will be the same
> as lc_collate, but for special applications it might be set differently.

max_function_args (integer)

> Reports the maximum number of function arguments. It is determined by
> the value of FUNC_MAX_ARGS when building the server. The default value is
> 100 arguments.

max_identifier_length (integer)

> Reports the maximum identifier length. It is determined as one less than
> the value of NAMEDATALEN when building the server. The default value
> of NAMEDATALEN is 64; therefore the default max_identifier_length is 63
> bytes.

max_index_keys (integer)

> Reports the maximum number of index keys. It is determined by the value
> of INDEX_MAX_KEYS when building the server. The default value is 32 keys.

server_encoding (string)

> Reports the database encoding (character set). It is determined when the
> database is created. Ordinarily, clients need only be concerned with the
> value of client_encoding.

`server_version` (`string`)

> Reports the version number of the server. It is determined by the value of
> `PG_VERSION` when building the server.

`server_version_num` (`integer`)

> Reports the version number of the server as an integer. It is determined
> by the value of `PG_VERSION_NUM` when building the server.

4.14 Customized Options

This feature was designed to allow parameters not normally known to PostgreSQL to be added by add-on modules (such as procedural languages). This
allows add-on modules to be configured in the standard ways.

`custom_variable_classes` (`string`)

> This variable specifies one or several class names to be used for custom
> variables, in the form of a comma-separated list. A custom variable is a
> variable not normally known to PostgreSQL proper but used by some add-
> on module. Such variables must have names consisting of a class name, a
> dot, and a variable name. `custom_variable_classes` specifies all the class
> names in use in a particular installation. This parameter can only be set
> in the 'postgresql.conf' file or on the server command line.

The difficulty with setting custom variables in 'postgresql.conf' is that
the file must be read before add-on modules have been loaded, and so custom
variables would ordinarily be rejected as unknown. When `custom_variable_`
`classes` is set, the server will accept definitions of arbitrary variables within
each specified class. These variables will be treated as placeholders and will
have no function until the module that defines them is loaded. When a module
for a specific class is loaded, it will add the proper variable definitions for its
class name, convert any placeholder values according to those definitions, and
issue warnings for any placeholders of its class that remain (which presumably
would be misspelled configuration variables).

Here is an example of what 'postgresql.conf' might contain when using
custom variables:

```
custom_variable_classes = 'plr,plperl'
plr.path = '/usr/lib/R'
plperl.use_strict = true
plruby.use_strict = true    # generates error: unknown
                              class name
```

4.15 Developer Options

The following parameters are intended for work on the PostgreSQL source, and in some cases to assist with recovery of severely damaged databases. There should be no reason to use them in a production database setup. As such, they have been excluded from the sample 'postgresql.conf' file. Note that many of these parameters require special source compilation flags to work at all.

allow_system_table_mods (boolean)
> Allows modification of the structure of system tables. This is used by initdb. This parameter can only be set at server start.

debug_assertions (boolean)
> Turns on various assertion checks. This is a debugging aid. If you are experiencing strange problems or crashes you might want to turn this on, as it might expose programming mistakes. To use this parameter, the macro USE_ASSERT_CHECKING must be defined when PostgreSQL is built (accomplished by the configure option --enable-cassert). Note that debug_assertions defaults to on if PostgreSQL has been built with assertions enabled.

ignore_system_indexes (boolean)
> Ignore system indexes when reading system tables (but still update the indexes when modifying the tables). This is useful when recovering from damaged system indexes. This parameter cannot be changed after session start.

post_auth_delay (integer)
> If nonzero, a delay of this many seconds occurs when a new server process is started, after it conducts the authentication procedure. This is intended to give an opportunity to attach to the server process with a debugger. This parameter cannot be changed after session start.

pre_auth_delay (integer)
> If nonzero, a delay of this many seconds occurs just after a new server process is forked, before it conducts the authentication procedure. This is intended to give an opportunity to attach to the server process with a debugger to trace down misbehavior in authentication. This parameter can only be set in the 'postgresql.conf' file or on the server command line.

trace_notify (boolean)
> Generates a great amount of debugging output for the LISTEN and NOTIFY commands. client_min_messages or log_min_messages must be DEBUG1 or lower to send this output to the client or server log, respectively.

trace_sort (boolean)
> If on, emit information about resource usage during sort operations. This parameter is only available if the TRACE_SORT macro was defined when PostgreSQL was compiled. (However, TRACE_SORT is currently defined by default.)

`trace_locks (boolean)`
`trace_lwlocks (boolean)`
`trace_userlocks (boolean)`
`trace_lock_oidmin (boolean)`
`trace_lock_table (boolean)`
`debug_deadlocks (boolean)`
`log_btree_build_stats (boolean)`
> Various other code tracing and debugging options.

`wal_debug (boolean)`
> If on, emit WAL-related debugging output. This parameter is only available if the `WAL_DEBUG` macro was defined when PostgreSQL was compiled.

`zero_damaged_pages (boolean)`
> Detection of a damaged page header normally causes PostgreSQL to report an error, aborting the current command. Setting `zero_damaged_pages` to on causes the system to instead report a warning, zero out the damaged page, and continue processing. This behavior *will destroy data*, namely all the rows on the damaged page. But it allows you to get past the error and retrieve rows from any undamaged pages that may be present in the table. So it is useful for recovering data if corruption has occurred due to hardware or software error. You should generally not set this on until you have given up hope of recovering data from the damaged page(s) of a table. The default setting is `off`, and it can only be changed by a superuser.

4.16 Short Options

For convenience there are also single letter command-line option switches available for some parameters. They are described in Table 4.1. Some of these options exist for historical reasons, and their presence as a single-letter option does not necessarily indicate an endorsement to use the option heavily.

SHORT OPTION	EQUIVALENT
-A x	debug_assertions = x
-B x	shared_buffers = x
-d x	log_min_messages = DEBUGx
-e	datestyle = euro
-fb, -fh, -fi, -fm, -fn, -fs, -ft	enable_bitmapscan = off, enable_hashjoin = off, enable_indexscan = off, enable_mergejoin = off, enable_nestloop = off, enable_seqscan = off, enable_tidscan = off
-F	fsync = off
-h x	listen_addresses = x
-i	listen_addresses = '*'
-k x	unix_socket_directory = x
-l	ssl = on
-N x	max_connections = x
-O	allow_system_table_mods = on
-p x	port = x
-P	ignore_system_indexes = on
-s	log_statement_stats = on
-S x	work_mem = x
-tpa, -tpl, -te	log_parser_stats = on, log_planner_stats = on, log_executor_stats = on
-W x	post_auth_delay = x

Table 4.1: Short option key

5 Database Roles and Privileges

PostgreSQL manages database access permissions using the concept of *roles*. A role can be thought of as either a database user, or a group of database users, depending on how the role is set up. Roles can own database objects (for example, tables) and can assign privileges on those objects to other roles to control who has access to which objects. Furthermore, it is possible to grant *membership* in a role to another role, thus allowing the member role use of privileges assigned to the role it is a member of.

The concept of roles subsumes the concepts of "users" and "groups". In PostgreSQL versions before 8.1, users and groups were distinct kinds of entities, but now there are only roles. Any role can act as a user, a group, or both.

This chapter describes how to create and manage roles and introduces the privilege system. More information about the various types of database objects and the effects of privileges can be found in Volume 1, Chapter 3 *Data Definition*.

5.1 Database Roles

Database roles are conceptually completely separate from operating system users. In practice it might be convenient to maintain a correspondence, but this is not required. Database roles are global across a database cluster installation (and not per individual database). To create a role use the CREATE ROLE SQL command:

        CREATE ROLE name;

name follows the rules for SQL identifiers: either unadorned without special characters, or double-quoted. (In practice, you will usually want to add additional options, such as LOGIN, to the command. More details appear below.) To remove an existing role, use the analogous DROP ROLE command:

        DROP ROLE name;

For convenience, the programs createuser and dropuser are provided as wrappers around these SQL commands that can be called from the shell command line:

        createuser name
        dropuser name

To determine the set of existing roles, examine the pg_roles system catalog, for example

        SELECT rolname FROM pg_roles;

The psql program's \du meta-command is also useful for listing the existing roles.

In order to bootstrap the database system, a freshly initialized system always contains one predefined role. This role is always a "superuser", and by default (unless altered when running initdb) it will have the same name as the operating system user that initialized the database cluster. Customarily, this role will be named postgres. In order to create more roles you first have to connect as this initial role.

Every connection to the database server is made in the name of some particular role, and this role determines the initial access privileges for commands issued on that connection. The role name to use for a particular database connection is indicated by the client that is initiating the connection request in an application-specific fashion. For example, the psql program uses the -U command line option to indicate the role to connect as. Many applications assume the name of the current operating system user by default (including createuser and psql). Therefore it is often convenient to maintain a naming correspondence between roles and operating system users.

The set of database roles a given client connection may connect as is determined by the client authentication setup, as explained in Chapter 7 *Client Authentication*, page 99. (Thus, a client is not necessarily limited to connect as the role with the same name as its operating system user, just as a person's login name need not match her real name.) Since the role identity determines the set of privileges available to a connected client, it is important to carefully configure this when setting up a multiuser environment.

5.2 Role Attributes

A database role may have a number of attributes that define its privileges and interact with the client authentication system.

login privilege
> Only roles that have the LOGIN attribute can be used as the initial role name for a database connection. A role with the LOGIN attribute can be considered the same thing as a "database user". To create a role with login privilege, use either
>
>> CREATE ROLE name LOGIN;
>> CREATE USER name;
>
> (CREATE USER is equivalent to CREATE ROLE except that CREATE USER assumes LOGIN by default, while CREATE ROLE does not.)

superuser status
> A database superuser bypasses all permission checks. This is a dangerous privilege and should not be used carelessly; it is best to do most of your work as a role that is not a superuser. To create a new database superuser, use CREATE ROLE name SUPERUSER. You must do this as a role that is already a superuser.

database creation
> A role must be explicitly given permission to create databases (except for superusers, since those bypass all permission checks). To create such a role, use CREATE ROLE name CREATEDB.

role creation
> A role must be explicitly given permission to create more roles (except for superusers, since those bypass all permission checks). To create such a role, use CREATE ROLE name CREATEROLE. A role with CREATEROLE privilege can alter and drop other roles, too, as well as grant or revoke membership in

them. However, to create, alter, drop, or change membership of a superuser
role, superuser status is required; CREATEROLE is not sufficient for that.

password

A password is only significant if the client authentication method requires the user to supply a password when connecting to the database.
The password, md5, and crypt authentication methods make use of passwords. Database passwords are separate from operating system passwords.
Specify a password upon role creation with CREATE ROLE *name* PASSWORD
'*string*'.

A role's attributes can be modified after creation with ALTER ROLE. See the
reference pages for the CREATE ROLE and ALTER ROLE commands for details.

> **Tip:** It is good practice to create a role that has the CREATEDB and
> CREATEROLE privileges, but is not a superuser, and then use this role
> for all routine management of databases and roles. This approach
> avoids the dangers of operating as a superuser for tasks that do not
> really require it.

A role can also have role-specific defaults for many of the run-time configuration settings described in Chapter 4 *Server Configuration*, page 45. For
example, if for some reason you want to disable index scans (hint: not a good
idea) anytime you connect, you can use

```
ALTER ROLE myname SET enable_indexscan TO off;
```

This will save the setting (but not set it immediately). In subsequent connections by this role it will appear as though SET enable_indexscan TO off; had
been executed just before the session started. You can still alter this setting
during the session; it will only be the default. To remove a role-specific default
setting, use ALTER ROLE *rolename* RESET *varname*;. Note that role-specific defaults attached to roles without LOGIN privilege are fairly useless, since they will
never be invoked.

5.3 Privileges

When an object is created, it is assigned an owner. The owner is normally
the role that executed the creation statement. For most kinds of objects, the
initial state is that only the owner (or a superuser) can do anything with the
object. To allow other roles to use it, *privileges* must be granted. There are several different kinds of privilege: SELECT, INSERT, UPDATE, DELETE, REFERENCES,
TRIGGER, CREATE, CONNECT, TEMPORARY, EXECUTE, and USAGE. For more information on the different types of privileges supported by PostgreSQL, see the GRANT
reference page.

To assign privileges, the GRANT command is used. So, if joe is an existing
role, and accounts is an existing table, the privilege to update the table can be
granted with

```
GRANT UPDATE ON accounts TO joe;
```
The special name PUBLIC can be used to grant a privilege to every role on the system. Writing ALL in place of a specific privilege specifies that all privileges that apply to the object will be granted.

To revoke a privilege, use the fittingly named REVOKE command:
```
REVOKE ALL ON accounts FROM PUBLIC;
```
The special privileges of an object's owner (i.e., the right to modify or destroy the object) are always implicit in being the owner, and cannot be granted or revoked. But the owner can choose to revoke his own ordinary privileges, for example to make a table read-only for himself as well as others.

An object can be assigned to a new owner with an ALTER command of the appropriate kind for the object. Superusers can always do this; ordinary roles can only do it if they are both the current owner of the object (or a member of the owning role) and a member of the new owning role.

5.4 Role Membership

It is frequently convenient to group users together to ease management of privileges: that way, privileges can be granted to, or revoked from, a group as a whole. In PostgreSQL this is done by creating a role that represents the group, and then granting *membership* in the group role to individual user roles.

To set up a group role, first create the role:
```
CREATE ROLE name;
```
Typically a role being used as a group would not have the LOGIN attribute, though you can set it if you wish.

Once the group role exists, you can add and remove members using the GRANT and REVOKE commands:
```
GRANT group_role TO role1, ... ;
REVOKE group_role FROM role1, ... ;
```
You can grant membership to other group roles, too (since there isn't really any distinction between group roles and non-group roles). The database will not let you set up circular membership loops. Also, it is not permitted to grant membership in a role to PUBLIC.

The members of a role can use the privileges of the group role in two ways. First, every member of a group can explicitly do SET ROLE to temporarily "become" the group role. In this state, the database session has access to the privileges of the group role rather than the original login role, and any database objects created are considered owned by the group role not the login role. Second, member roles that have the INHERIT attribute automatically have use of privileges of roles they are members of. As an example, suppose we have done
```
CREATE ROLE joe LOGIN INHERIT;
CREATE ROLE admin NOINHERIT;
CREATE ROLE wheel NOINHERIT;
GRANT admin TO joe;
GRANT wheel TO admin;
```

Immediately after connecting as role joe, a database session will have use of privileges granted directly to joe plus any privileges granted to admin, because joe "inherits" admin's privileges. However, privileges granted to wheel are not available, because even though joe is indirectly a member of wheel, the membership is via admin which has the NOINHERIT attribute. After

```
SET ROLE admin;
```

the session would have use of only those privileges granted to admin, and not those granted to joe. After

```
SET ROLE wheel;
```

the session would have use of only those privileges granted to wheel, and not those granted to either joe or admin. The original privilege state can be restored with any of

```
SET ROLE joe;
SET ROLE NONE;
RESET ROLE;
```

Note: The SET ROLE command always allows selecting any role that the original login role is directly or indirectly a member of. Thus, in the above example, it is not necessary to become admin before becoming wheel.

Note: In the SQL standard, there is a clear distinction between users and roles, and users do not automatically inherit privileges while roles do. This behavior can be obtained in PostgreSQL by giving roles being used as SQL roles the INHERIT attribute, while giving roles being used as SQL users the NOINHERIT attribute. However, PostgreSQL defaults to giving all roles the INHERIT attribute, for backwards compatibility with pre-8.1 releases in which users always had use of permissions granted to groups they were members of.

The role attributes LOGIN, SUPERUSER, CREATEDB, and CREATEROLE can be thought of as special privileges, but they are never inherited as ordinary privileges on database objects are. You must actually SET ROLE to a specific role having one of these attributes in order to make use of the attribute. Continuing the above example, we might well choose to grant CREATEDB and CREATEROLE to the admin role. Then a session connecting as role joe would not have these privileges immediately, only after doing SET ROLE admin.

To destroy a group role, use DROP ROLE:

```
DROP ROLE name;
```

Any memberships in the group role are automatically revoked (but the member roles are not otherwise affected). Note however that any objects owned by the group role must first be dropped or reassigned to other owners; and any permissions granted to the group role must be revoked.

5.5 Functions and Triggers

Functions and triggers allow users to insert code into the backend server that other users may execute unintentionally. Hence, both mechanisms permit users to "Trojan horse" others with relative ease. The only real protection is tight control over who can define functions.

Functions run inside the backend server process with the operating system permissions of the database server daemon. If the programming language used for the function allows unchecked memory accesses, it is possible to change the server's internal data structures. Hence, among many other things, such functions can circumvent any system access controls. Function languages that allow such access are considered "untrusted", and PostgreSQL allows only superusers to create functions written in those languages.

6 Managing Databases

Every instance of a running PostgreSQL server manages one or more databases. Databases are therefore the topmost hierarchical level for organizing SQL objects ("database objects"). This chapter describes the properties of databases, and how to create, manage, and destroy them.

6.1 Overview

A database is a named collection of SQL objects ("database objects"). Generally, every database object (tables, functions, etc.) belongs to one and only one database. (But there are a few system catalogs, for example pg_database, that belong to a whole cluster and are accessible from each database within the cluster.) More accurately, a database is a collection of schemas and the schemas contain the tables, functions, etc. So the full hierarchy is: server, database, schema, table (or some other kind of object, such as a function).

When connecting to the database server, a client must specify in its connection request the name of the database it wants to connect to. It is not possible to access more than one database per connection. (But an application is not restricted in the number of connections it opens to the same or other databases.) Databases are physically separated and access control is managed at the connection level. If one PostgreSQL server instance is to house projects or users that should be separate and for the most part unaware of each other, it is therefore recommendable to put them into separate databases. If the projects or users are interrelated and should be able to use each other's resources they should be put in the same database, but possibly into separate schemas. Schemas are a purely logical structure and who can access what is managed by the privilege system. More information about managing schemas is in Volume 1, Section 3.7 *Schemas*.

Databases are created with the CREATE DATABASE command (see Section 6.2 *Creating a Database*, page 94) and destroyed with the DROP DATABASE command (see Section 6.5 *Destroying a Database*, page 96). To determine the set of existing databases, examine the pg_database system catalog, for example

    SELECT datname FROM pg_database;

The psql program's \l meta-command and -l command-line option are also useful for listing the existing databases.

> **Note:** The SQL standard calls databases "catalogs", but there is no difference in practice.

6.2 Creating a Database

In order to create a database, the PostgreSQL server must be up and running (see Section 3.3 *Starting the Database Server*, page 28).

Databases are created with the SQL command CREATE DATABASE:

    CREATE DATABASE name ;

where *name* follows the usual rules for SQL identifiers. The current role automatically becomes the owner of the new database. It is the privilege of the owner of a database to remove it later on (which also removes all the objects in it, even if they have a different owner).

The creation of databases is a restricted operation. See Section 5.2 *Role Attributes*, page 88 for how to grant permission.

Since you need to be connected to the database server in order to execute the CREATE DATABASE command, the question remains how the *first* database at any given site can be created. The first database is always created by the initdb command when the data storage area is initialized. (See Section 3.2 *Creating a Database Cluster*, page 27.) This database is called postgres. So to create the first "ordinary" database you can connect to postgres.

A second database, template1, is also created by initdb. Whenever a new database is created within the cluster, template1 is essentially cloned. This means that any changes you make in template1 are propagated to all subsequently created databases. Therefore it is unwise to use template1 for real work, but when used judiciously this feature can be convenient. More details appear in Section 6.3 *Template Databases*, page 95.

As a convenience, there is a program that you can execute from the shell to create new databases, createdb.

    createdb dbname

createdb does no magic. It connects to the postgres database and issues the CREATE DATABASE command, exactly as described above. The createdb reference page contains the invocation details. Note that createdb without any arguments will create a database with the current user name, which may or may not be what you want.

> **Note:** Chapter 7 *Client Authentication*, page 99 contains information about how to restrict who can connect to a given database.

Sometimes you want to create a database for someone else. That role should become the owner of the new database, so he can configure and manage it himself. To achieve that, use one of the following commands:

    CREATE DATABASE dbname OWNER rolename;

from the SQL environment, or

    createdb -O rolename dbname

from the shell. You must be a superuser to be allowed to create a database for someone else (that is, for a role you are not a member of).

6.3 Template Databases

CREATE DATABASE actually works by copying an existing database. By default, it copies the standard system database named template1. Thus that database is the "template" from which new databases are made. If you add objects to template1, these objects will be copied into subsequently created user databases. This behavior allows site-local modifications to the standard set of objects in databases. For example, if you install the procedural language PL/pgSQL in template1, it will automatically be available in user databases without any extra action being taken when those databases are made.

There is a second standard system database named template0. This database contains the same data as the initial contents of template1, that is, only the standard objects predefined by your version of PostgreSQL. template0 should never be changed after initdb. By instructing CREATE DATABASE to copy template0 instead of template1, you can create a "virgin" user database that contains none of the site-local additions in template1. This is particularly handy when restoring a pg_dump dump: the dump script should be restored in a virgin database to ensure that one recreates the correct contents of the dumped database, without any conflicts with additions that may now be present in template1.

To create a database by copying template0, use

```
CREATE DATABASE dbname TEMPLATE template0;
```
from the SQL environment, or

```
createdb -T template0 dbname
```
from the shell.

It is possible to create additional template databases, and indeed one may copy any database in a cluster by specifying its name as the template for CREATE DATABASE. It is important to understand, however, that this is not (yet) intended as a general-purpose "COPY DATABASE" facility. The principal limitation is that no other sessions can be connected to the source database while it is being copied. CREATE DATABASE will fail if any other connection exists when it starts; otherwise, new connections to the source database are locked out until CREATE DATABASE completes.

Two useful flags exist in pg_database for each database: the columns datistemplate and datallowconn. datistemplate may be set to indicate that a database is intended as a template for CREATE DATABASE. If this flag is set, the database may be cloned by any user with CREATEDB privileges; if it is not set, only superusers and the owner of the database may clone it. If datallowconn is false, then no new connections to that database will be allowed (but existing sessions are not killed simply by setting the flag false). The template0 database is normally marked datallowconn = false to prevent modification of it. Both template0 and template1 should always be marked with datistemplate = true.

> Note: template1 and template0 do not have any special status beyond the fact that the name template1 is the default source database name for CREATE DATABASE. For example, one could drop template1 and recreate it from template0 without any ill effects. This course of

action might be advisable if one has carelessly added a bunch of junk in template1. (To delete template1, it must have datistemplate = false.)

The postgres database is also created when a database cluster is initialized. This database is meant as a default database for users and applications to connect to. It is simply a copy of template1 and may be dropped and recreated if required.

6.4 Database Configuration

Recall from Chapter 4 *Server Configuration*, page 45 that the PostgreSQL server provides a large number of run-time configuration variables. You can set database-specific default values for many of these settings.

For example, if for some reason you want to disable the GEQO optimizer for a given database, you'd ordinarily have to either disable it for all databases or make sure that every connecting client is careful to issue SET geqo TO off;. To make this setting the default within a particular database, you can execute the command

    ALTER DATABASE mydb SET geqo TO off;

This will save the setting (but not set it immediately). In subsequent connections to this database it will appear as though SET geqo TO off; had been executed just before the session started. Note that users can still alter this setting during their sessions; it will only be the default. To undo any such setting, use ALTER DATABASE dbname RESET varname;.

6.5 Destroying a Database

Databases are destroyed with the command DROP DATABASE:

    DROP DATABASE name;

Only the owner of the database, or a superuser, can drop a database. Dropping a database removes all objects that were contained within the database. The destruction of a database cannot be undone.

You cannot execute the DROP DATABASE command while connected to the victim database. You can, however, be connected to any other database, including the template1 database. template1 would be the only option for dropping the last user database of a given cluster.

For convenience, there is also a shell program to drop databases, dropdb:

    dropdb dbname

(Unlike createdb, it is not the default action to drop the database with the current user name.)

6.6 Tablespaces

Tablespaces in PostgreSQL allow database administrators to define locations in the file system where the files representing database objects can be stored. Once created, a tablespace can be referred to by name when creating database objects.

By using tablespaces, an administrator can control the disk layout of a PostgreSQL installation. This is useful in at least two ways. First, if the partition or volume on which the cluster was initialized runs out of space and cannot be extended, a tablespace can be created on a different partition and used until the system can be reconfigured.

Second, tablespaces allow an administrator to use knowledge of the usage pattern of database objects to optimize performance. For example, an index which is very heavily used can be placed on a very fast, highly available disk, such as an expensive solid state device. At the same time a table storing archived data which is rarely used or not performance critical could be stored on a less expensive, slower disk system.

To define a tablespace, use the CREATE TABLESPACE command, for example:

```
CREATE TABLESPACE fastspace LOCATION '/mnt/sda1/postgresql/data';
```

The location must be an existing, empty directory that is owned by the PostgreSQL system user. All objects subsequently created within the tablespace will be stored in files underneath this directory.

> **Note:** There is usually not much point in making more than one tablespace per logical file system, since you cannot control the location of individual files within a logical file system. However, PostgreSQL does not enforce any such limitation, and indeed it is not directly aware of the file system boundaries on your system. It just stores files in the directories you tell it to use.

Creation of the tablespace itself must be done as a database superuser, but after that you can allow ordinary database users to make use of it. To do that, grant them the CREATE privilege on it.

Tables, indexes, and entire databases can be assigned to particular tablespaces. To do so, a user with the CREATE privilege on a given tablespace must pass the tablespace name as a parameter to the relevant command. For example, the following creates a table in the tablespace space1:

```
CREATE TABLE foo(i int) TABLESPACE space1;
```

Alternatively, use the default_tablespace parameter:

```
SET default_tablespace = space1;
CREATE TABLE foo(i int);
```

When default_tablespace is set to anything but an empty string, it supplies an implicit TABLESPACE clause for CREATE TABLE and CREATE INDEX commands that do not have an explicit one.

The tablespace associated with a database is used to store the system catalogs of that database, as well as any temporary files created by server processes using that database. Furthermore, it is the default tablespace selected for tables and indexes created within the database, if no TABLESPACE clause is given (either explicitly or via default_tablespace) when the objects are created. If a database is created without specifying a tablespace for it, it uses the same tablespace as the template database it is copied from.

Two tablespaces are automatically created by initdb. The pg_global tablespace is used for shared system catalogs. The pg_default tablespace is the default tablespace of the template1 and template0 databases (and, therefore, will be the default tablespace for other databases as well, unless overridden by a TABLESPACE clause in CREATE DATABASE).

Once created, a tablespace can be used from any database, provided the requesting user has sufficient privilege. This means that a tablespace cannot be dropped until all objects in all databases using the tablespace have been removed.

To remove an empty tablespace, use the DROP TABLESPACE command.

To determine the set of existing tablespaces, examine the pg_tablespace system catalog, for example

    SELECT spcname FROM pg_tablespace;

The psql program's \db meta-command is also useful for listing the existing tablespaces.

PostgreSQL makes extensive use of symbolic links to simplify the implementation of tablespaces. This means that tablespaces can be used *only* on systems that support symbolic links.

The directory '$PGDATA/pg_tblspc' contains symbolic links that point to each of the non-built-in tablespaces defined in the cluster. Although not recommended, it is possible to adjust the tablespace layout by hand by redefining these links. Two warnings: do not do so while the server is running; and after you restart the server, update the pg_tablespace catalog to show the new locations. (If you do not, pg_dump will continue to show the old tablespace locations.)

7 Client Authentication

When a client application connects to the database server, it specifies which PostgreSQL database user name it wants to connect as, much the same way one logs into a Unix computer as a particular user. Within the SQL environment the active database user name determines access privileges to database objects—see Chapter 5 *Database Roles and Privileges*, page 87 for more information. Therefore, it is essential to restrict which database users can connect.

> **Note:** As explained in Chapter 5 *Database Roles and Privileges*, page 87, PostgreSQL actually does privilege management in terms of "roles". In this chapter, we consistently use *database user* to mean "role with the LOGIN privilege".

Authentication is the process by which the database server establishes the identity of the client, and by extension determines whether the client application (or the user who runs the client application) is permitted to connect with the database user name that was requested.

PostgreSQL offers a number of different client authentication methods. The method used to authenticate a particular client connection can be selected on the basis of (client) host address, database, and user.

PostgreSQL database user names are logically separate from user names of the operating system in which the server runs. If all the users of a particular server also have accounts on the server's machine, it makes sense to assign database user names that match their operating system user names. However, a server that accepts remote connections may have many database users who have no local operating system account, and in such cases there need be no connection between database user names and OS user names.

7.1 The pg_hba.conf file

Client authentication is controlled by a configuration file, which traditionally is named 'pg_hba.conf' and is stored in the database cluster's data directory. (HBA stands for host-based authentication.) A default 'pg_hba.conf' file is installed when the data directory is initialized by initdb. It is possible to place the authentication configuration file elsewhere, however; see the hba_file configuration parameter.

The general format of the 'pg_hba.conf' file is a set of records, one per line. Blank lines are ignored, as is any text after the # comment character. A record is made up of a number of fields which are separated by spaces and/or tabs. Fields can contain white space if the field value is quoted. Records cannot be continued across lines.

Each record specifies a connection type, a client IP address range (if relevant for the connection type), a database name, a user name, and the authentication method to be used for connections matching these parameters. The first record with a matching connection type, client address, requested database, and user name is used to perform authentication. There is no "fall-through" or "backup":

if one record is chosen and the authentication fails, subsequent records are not considered. If no record matches, access is denied.

A record may have one of the seven formats

```
local database user auth-method [auth-option]
host database user CIDR-address auth-method [auth-option]
hostssl database user CIDR-address auth-method [auth-option]
hostnossl database user CIDR-address auth-method [auth-option]
host database user IP-address IP-mask auth-method [auth-option]
hostssl database user IP-address IP-mask auth-method
 [auth-option]
hostnossl database user IP-address IP-mask auth-method
 [auth-option]
```

Note that each record should be a single line (in the table above, the last two lines have been wrapped). The meaning of the fields is as follows:

local
> This record matches connection attempts using Unix-domain sockets. Without a record of this type, Unix-domain socket connections are disallowed.

host
> This record matches connection attempts made using TCP/IP. host records match either SSL or non-SSL connection attempts.

>> Note: Remote TCP/IP connections will not be possible unless the server is started with an appropriate value for the listen_addresses configuration parameter, since the default behavior is to listen for TCP/IP connections only on the local loopback address localhost.

hostssl
> This record matches connection attempts made using TCP/IP, but only when the connection is made with SSL encryption.

> To make use of this option the server must be built with SSL support. Furthermore, SSL must be enabled at server start time by setting the ssl configuration parameter (see Section 3.7 *Secure TCP/IP Connections with SSL*, page 42 for more information).

hostnossl
> This record type has the opposite logic to hostssl: it only matches connection attempts made over TCP/IP that do not use SSL.

database
> Specifies which database names this record matches. The value all specifies that it matches all databases. The value sameuser specifies that the record matches if the requested database has the same name as the requested user. The value samerole specifies that the requested user must be a member of the role with the same name as the requested database. (samegroup is an obsolete but still accepted spelling of samerole.) Otherwise, this is the name of a specific PostgreSQL database. Multiple database

names can be supplied by separating them with commas. A separate file
containing database names can be specified by preceding the file name with
@.

user

Specifies which database user names this record matches. The value all
specifies that it matches all users. Otherwise, this is either the name of
a specific database user, or a group name preceded by +. (Recall that
there is no real distinction between users and groups in PostgreSQL; a +
mark really means "match any of the roles that are directly or indirectly
members of this role", while a name without a + mark matches only that
specific role.) Multiple user names can be supplied by separating them
with commas. A separate file containing user names can be specified by
preceding the file name with @.

CIDR-address

Specifies the client machine IP address range that this record matches. It
contains an IP address in standard dotted decimal notation and a CIDR
mask length. (IP addresses can only be specified numerically, not as do-
main or host names.) The mask length indicates the number of high-order
bits of the client IP address that must match. Bits to the right of this
must be zero in the given IP address. There must not be any white space
between the IP address, the /, and the CIDR mask length.

Typical examples of a *CIDR-address* are 172.20.143.89/32 for a single
host, or 172.20.143.0/24 for a small network, or 10.6.0.0/16 for a larger
one. To specify a single host, use a CIDR mask of 32 for IPv4 or 128 for
IPv6. In a network address, do not omit trailing zeroes.

An IP address given in IPv4 format will match IPv6 connections that have
the corresponding address, for example 127.0.0.1 will match the IPv6
address ::ffff:127.0.0.1. An entry given in IPv6 format will match
only IPv6 connections, even if the represented address is in the IPv4-in-
IPv6 range. Note that entries in IPv6 format will be rejected if the system's
C library does not have support for IPv6 addresses.

This field only applies to host, hostssl, and hostnossl records.

IP-address
IP-mask

These fields may be used as an alternative to the *CIDR-address* notation.
Instead of specifying the mask length, the actual mask is specified in a
separate column. For example, 255.0.0.0 represents an IPv4 CIDR mask
length of 8, and 255.255.255.255 represents a CIDR mask length of 32.

These fields only apply to host, hostssl, and hostnossl records.

auth-method

Specifies the authentication method to use when connecting via this record.
The possible choices are summarized here; details are in Section 7.2 *Authentication methods*, page 105.

trust

> Allow the connection unconditionally. This method allows anyone that can connect to the PostgreSQL database server to login as any PostgreSQL user they like, without the need for a password. See Section 7.2.1 *Trust authentication*, page 105 for details.

reject

> Reject the connection unconditionally. This is useful for "filtering out" certain hosts from a group.

md5

> Require the client to supply an MD5-encrypted password for authentication. See Section 7.2.2 *Password authentication*, page 106 for details.

crypt

> **Note:** This option is recommended only for communicating with pre-7.2 clients.

> Require the client to supply a crypt()-encrypted password for authentication. md5 is now recommended over crypt. See Section 7.2.2 *Password authentication*, page 106 for details.

password

> Require the client to supply an unencrypted password for authentication. Since the password is sent in clear text over the network, this should not be used on untrusted networks. It also does not usually work with threaded client applications. See Section 7.2.2 *Password authentication*, page 106 for details.

krb5

> Use Kerberos V5 to authenticate the user. This is only available for TCP/IP connections. See Section 7.2.3 *Kerberos authentication*, page 106 for details.

ident

> Obtain the operating system user name of the client (for TCP/IP connections by contacting the ident server on the client, for local connections by getting it from the operating system) and check if the user is allowed to connect as the requested database user by consulting the map specified after the ident key word. See Section 7.2.4 *Ident-based authentication*, page 107 for details.

ldap

> Authenticate using LDAP to a central server. See Section 7.2.5 *LDAP authentication*, page 109 for details.

pam

> Authenticate using the Pluggable Authentication Modules (PAM) service provided by the operating system. See Section 7.2.6 *PAM authentication*, page 110 for details.

auth-option

> The meaning of this optional field depends on the chosen authentication method. Details appear below.

Files included by @ constructs are read as lists of names, which can be separated by either whitespace or commas. Comments are introduced by #, just as in 'pg_hba.conf', and nested @ constructs are allowed. Unless the file name following @ is an absolute path, it is taken to be relative to the directory containing the referencing file.

Since the 'pg_hba.conf' records are examined sequentially for each connection attempt, the order of the records is significant. Typically, earlier records will have tight connection match parameters and weaker authentication methods, while later records will have looser match parameters and stronger authentication methods. For example, one might wish to use trust authentication for local TCP/IP connections but require a password for remote TCP/IP connections. In this case a record specifying trust authentication for connections from 127.0.0.1 would appear before a record specifying password authentication for a wider range of allowed client IP addresses.

The 'pg_hba.conf' file is read on start-up and when the main server process receives a SIGHUP signal. If you edit the file on an active system, you will need to signal the server (using pg_ctl reload or kill -HUP) to make it re-read the file.

> **Tip:** To connect to a particular database, a user must not only pass the 'pg_hba.conf' checks, but must have the CONNECT privilege for the database. If you wish to restrict which users can connect to which databases, it's usually easier to control this by granting/revoking CONNECT privilege than to put the rules into 'pg_hba.conf' entries.

Some examples of 'pg_hba.conf' entries are shown in *Example pg_hba.conf entries*. See the next section for details on the different authentication methods.

Example pg_hba.conf entries:

```
# Allow any user on the local system to connect to any
# database under any database user name using
# Unix-domain sockets (the default for local
# connections).
#
# TYPE  DATABASE    USER        CIDR-ADDRESS        METHOD
local   all         all                             trust

# The same using local loopback TCP/IP connections.
#
# TYPE  DATABASE    USER        CIDR-ADDRESS        METHOD
host    all         all         127.0.0.1/32        trust

# The same as the last line but using a separate
# netmask column
#
# TYPE DATABASE USER IP-ADDRESS IP-MASK METHOD
host all all 127.0.0.1 255.255.255.255 trust
```

```
# Allow any user from any host with IP address
# 192.168.93.x to connect to database "postgres" as the
# same user name that ident reports for the connection
# (typically the Unix user name).
#
# TYPE  DATABASE    USER       CIDR-ADDRESS        METHOD
host postgres all 192.168.93.0/24 ident sameuser


# Allow a user from host 192.168.12.10 to connect to
# database "postgres" if the user's password is
# correctly supplied.
#
# TYPE  DATABASE    USER       CIDR-ADDRESS        METHOD
host    postgres    all        192.168.12.10/32    md5


# In the absence of preceding "host" lines, these two
# lines will reject all connection from 192.168.54.1
# (since that entry will be matched first), but allow
# Kerberos 5 connections from anywhere else on the
# Internet. The zero mask means that no bits of the
# host IP address are considered so it matches any
# host.
#
# TYPE  DATABASE    USER       CIDR-ADDRESS        METHOD
host    all         all        192.168.54.1/32     reject
host    all         all        0.0.0.0/0           krb5


# Allow users from 192.168.x.x hosts to connect to any
# database, if they pass the ident check. If, for
# example, ident says the user is "bryanh" and he
# requests to connect as PostgreSQL user "guest1", the
# connection is allowed if there is an entry in
# pg_ident.conf for map "omicron" that says "bryanh" is
# allowed to connect as "guest1".
#
# TYPE  DATABASE    USER       CIDR-ADDRESS        METHOD
host all all 192.168.0.0/16 ident omicron


# If these are the only three lines for local
# connections, they will allow local users to connect
# only to their own databases (databases with the same
# name as their database user name) except for
# administrators and members of role "support", who may
# connect to all databases. The file $PGDATA/admins
# contains a list of names of administrators. Passwords
# are required in all cases.
#
```

```
# TYPE   DATABASE     USER           CIDR-ADDRESS          METHOD
local    sameuser     all                                  md5
local    all          @admins                              md5
local    all          +support                             md5

# The last two lines above can be combined into a
# single line:
local    all          @admins,+support                     md5

# The database column can also use lists and file
# names:
local    db1,db2,@demodbs  all                             md5
```

7.2 Authentication methods

The following subsections describe the authentication methods in more detail.

7.2.1 Trust authentication

When trust authentication is specified, PostgreSQL assumes that anyone who can connect to the server is authorized to access the database with whatever database user name they specify (including superusers). Of course, restrictions made in the database and user columns still apply. This method should only be used when there is adequate operating-system-level protection on connections to the server.

trust authentication is appropriate and very convenient for local connections on a single-user workstation. It is usually *not* appropriate by itself on a multiuser machine. However, you may be able to use trust even on a multiuser machine, if you restrict access to the server's Unix-domain socket file using file-system permissions. To do this, set the unix_socket_permissions (and possibly unix_socket_group) configuration parameters as described in Section 4.3 *Connections and Authentication*, page 48. Or you could set the unix_socket_directory configuration parameter to place the socket file in a suitably restricted directory.

Setting file-system permissions only helps for Unix-socket connections. Local TCP/IP connections are not restricted by it; therefore, if you want to use file-system permissions for local security, remove the host ... 127.0.0.1 ... line from 'pg_hba.conf', or change it to a non-trust authentication method.

trust authentication is only suitable for TCP/IP connections if you trust every user on every machine that is allowed to connect to the server by the 'pg_hba.conf' lines that specify trust. It is seldom reasonable to use trust for any TCP/IP connections other than those from localhost (127.0.0.1).

7.2.2 Password authentication

The password-based authentication methods are md5, crypt, and password. These methods operate similarly except for the way that the password is sent across the connection: respectively, MD5-hashed, crypt-encrypted, and cleartext. A limitation is that the crypt method does not work with passwords that have been encrypted in pg_authid.

If you are at all concerned about password "sniffing" attacks then md5 is preferred, with crypt to be used only if you must support pre-7.2 clients. Plain password should be avoided especially for connections over the open Internet (unless you use SSL, SSH, or another communications security wrapper around the connection).

PostgreSQL database passwords are separate from operating system user passwords. The password for each database user is stored in the pg_authid system catalog. Passwords can be managed with the SQL commands CREATE USER and ALTER USER, e.g., CREATE USER foo WITH PASSWORD 'secret';. By default, that is, if no password has been set up, the stored password is null and password authentication will always fail for that user.

7.2.3 Kerberos authentication

Kerberos is an industry-standard secure authentication system suitable for distributed computing over a public network. A description of the Kerberos system is far beyond the scope of this document; in full generality it can be quite complex (yet powerful). The Kerberos FAQ[1] or MIT Kerberos page[2] can be good starting points for exploration. Several sources for Kerberos distributions exist. Kerberos provides secure authentication but does not encrypt queries or data passed over the network; for that use SSL.

PostgreSQL supports Kerberos version 5. Kerberos support has to be enabled when PostgreSQL is built; see Chapter 1 *Installation Instructions*, page 5 for more information.

PostgreSQL operates like a normal Kerberos service. The name of the service principal is *servicename/hostname@realm*.

servicename can be set on the server side using the krb_srvname configuration parameter, and on the client side using the krbsrvname connection parameter. (See also Volume 2, Section 1.1 *Database Connection Control Functions*.) The installation default can be changed from the default postgres at build time using ./configure --with-krb-srvnam=whatever. In most environments, this parameter never needs to be changed. However, to support multiple PostgreSQL installations on the same host it is necessary. Some Kerberos implementations may also require a different service name, such as Microsoft Active Directory which requires the service name to be in uppercase (POSTGRES).

hostname is the fully qualified host name of the server machine. The service principal's realm is the preferred realm of the server machine.

---

[1] http://www.nrl.navy.mil/CCS/people/kenh/kerberos-faq.html
[2] http://web.mit.edu/kerberos/www/

Client principals must have their PostgreSQL database user name as their first component, for example pgusername/otherstuff@realm. At present the realm of the client is not checked by PostgreSQL; so if you have cross-realm authentication enabled, then any principal in any realm that can communicate with yours will be accepted.

Make sure that your server keytab file is readable (and preferably only readable) by the PostgreSQL server account. (See also Section 3.1 *The PostgreSQL User Account*, page 27.) The location of the key file is specified by the krb_server_keyfile configuration parameter. The default is '/usr/local/pgsql/etc/krb5.keytab' (or whichever directory was specified as sysconfdir at build time).

The keytab file is generated by the Kerberos software; see the Kerberos documentation for details. The following example is for MIT-compatible Kerberos 5 implementations:

```
kadmin% ank -randkey postgres/server.my.domain.org
kadmin% ktadd -k krb5.keytab postgres/server.my.domain.org
```

When connecting to the database make sure you have a ticket for a principal matching the requested database user name. For example, for database user name fred, both principal fred@EXAMPLE.COM and fred/users.example.com@EXAMPLE.COM could be used to authenticate to the database server.

If you use mod_auth_kerb[3] and mod_perl on your Apache web server, you can use AuthType KerberosV5SaveCredentials with a mod_perl script. This gives secure database access over the web, no extra passwords required.

7.2.4 Ident-based authentication

The ident authentication method works by obtaining the client's operating system user name, then determining the allowed database user names using a map file that lists the permitted corresponding pairs of names. The determination of the client's user name is the security-critical point, and it works differently depending on the connection type.

7.2.4.1 Ident Authentication over TCP/IP

The "Identification Protocol" is described in *RFC 1413*. Virtually every Unix-like operating system ships with an ident server that listens on TCP port 113 by default. The basic functionality of an ident server is to answer questions like "What user initiated the connection that goes out of your port X and connects to my port Y?". Since PostgreSQL knows both X and Y when a physical connection is established, it can interrogate the ident server on the host of the connecting client and could theoretically determine the operating system user for any given connection this way.

The drawback of this procedure is that it depends on the integrity of the client: if the client machine is untrusted or compromised an attacker could run just about any program on port 113 and return any user name he chooses. This

---

[3] http://modauthkerb.sf.net

authentication method is therefore only appropriate for closed networks where each client machine is under tight control and where the database and system administrators operate in close contact. In other words, you must trust the machine running the ident server. Heed the warning:

> The Identification Protocol is not intended as an authorization or access control protocol.

— RFC 1413

Some ident servers have a nonstandard option that causes the returned user name to be encrypted, using a key that only the originating machine's administrator knows. This option *must not* be used when using the ident server with PostgreSQL, since PostgreSQL does not have any way to decrypt the returned string to determine the actual user name.

7.2.4.2 Ident Authentication over Local Sockets

On systems supporting SO_PEERCRED requests for Unix-domain sockets (currently Linux, FreeBSD, NetBSD, OpenBSD, and BSD/OS), ident authentication can also be applied to local connections. In this case, no security risk is added by using ident authentication; indeed it is a preferable choice for local connections on such systems.

On systems without SO_PEERCRED requests, ident authentication is only available for TCP/IP connections. As a work-around, it is possible to specify the localhost address 127.0.0.1 and make connections to this address. This method is trustworthy to the extent that you trust the local ident server.

7.2.4.3 Ident Maps

When using ident-based authentication, after having determined the name of the operating system user that initiated the connection, PostgreSQL checks whether that user is allowed to connect as the database user he is requesting to connect as. This is controlled by the ident map argument that follows the ident key word in the 'pg_hba.conf' file. There is a predefined ident map sameuser, which allows any operating system user to connect as the database user of the same name (if the latter exists). Other maps must be created manually.

Ident maps other than sameuser are defined in the ident map file, which by default is named 'pg_ident.conf' and is stored in the cluster's data directory. (It is possible to place the map file elsewhere, however; see the ident_file configuration parameter.) The ident map file contains lines of the general form:

    map-name ident-username database-username

Comments and whitespace are handled in the same way as in 'pg_hba.conf'. The map-name is an arbitrary name that will be used to refer to this mapping in 'pg_hba.conf'. The other two fields specify which operating system user is allowed to connect as which database user. The same map-name can be used repeatedly to specify more user-mappings within a single map. There is no restriction regarding how many database users a given operating system user may correspond to, nor vice versa.

The 'pg_ident.conf' file is read on start-up and when the main server process receives a SIGHUP signal. If you edit the file on an active system, you will need to signal the server (using pg_ctl reload or kill -HUP) to make it re-read the file.

A 'pg_ident.conf' file that could be used in conjunction with the 'pg_hba.conf' file in *Example pg_hba.conf entries*, page 103 is shown in *An example pg_ident.conf file*. In this example setup, anyone logged in to a machine on the 192.168 network that does not have the Unix user name bryanh, ann, or robert would not be granted access. Unix user robert would only be allowed access when he tries to connect as PostgreSQL user bob, not as robert or anyone else. ann would only be allowed to connect as ann. User bryanh would be allowed to connect as either bryanh himself or as guest1.

An example pg_ident.conf file:

```
# MAPNAME      IDENT-USERNAME      PG-USERNAME

omicron        bryanh              bryanh
omicron        ann                 ann
# bob has user name robert on these machines
omicron        robert              bob
# bryanh can also connect as guest1
omicron        bryanh              guest1
```

7.2.5 LDAP authentication

This authentication method operates similarly to password except that it uses LDAP as the authentication method. LDAP is used only to validate the user name/password pairs. Therefore the user must already exist in the database before LDAP can be used for authentication. The server and parameters used are specified after the ldap key word in the file 'pg_hba.conf'. The format of this parameter is:

```
ldap[s]://servername[:port]/base dn[;prefix[;suffix]]
```

Commas are used to specify multiple items in an ldap component. However, because unquoted commas are treated as item separators in 'pg_hba.conf', it is wise to double-quote the ldap URL to preserve any commas present, e.g.:

```
"ldap://ldap.example.net/dc=example,dc=net;EXAMPLE\"
```

If ldaps is specified instead of ldap, TLS encryption will be enabled for the connection. Note that this will encrypt only the connection between the PostgreSQL server and the LDAP server. The connection between the client and the PostgreSQL server is not affected by this setting. To make use of TLS encryption, you may need to configure the LDAP library prior to configuring PostgreSQL. Note that encrypted LDAP is available only if the platform's LDAP library supports it.

If no port is specified, the default port as configured in the LDAP library will be used.

The server will bind to the distinguished name specified as *base dn* using the user name supplied by the client. If *prefix* and *suffix* is specified, it will be prepended and appended to the user name before the bind. Typically, the prefix parameter is used to specify *cn=*, or *DOMAIN* in an Active Directory environment.

7.2.6 PAM authentication

This authentication method operates similarly to password except that it uses PAM (Pluggable Authentication Modules) as the authentication mechanism. The default PAM service name is postgresql. You can optionally supply your own service name after the pam key word in the file 'pg_hba.conf'. PAM is used only to validate user name/password pairs. Therefore the user must already exist in the database before PAM can be used for authentication. For more information about PAM, please read the Linux-PAM Page[4] and the Solaris PAM Page[5].

7.3 Authentication problems

Genuine authentication failures and related problems generally manifest themselves through error messages like the following.

```
FATAL:  no pg_hba.conf entry for host "123.123.123.123", user
 "andym", database "testdb"
```

This is what you are most likely to get if you succeed in contacting the server, but it does not want to talk to you. As the message suggests, the server refused the connection request because it found no matching entry in its 'pg_hba.conf' configuration file.

```
FATAL:  Password authentication failed for user "andym"
```

Messages like this indicate that you contacted the server, and it is willing to talk to you, but not until you pass the authorization method specified in the 'pg_hba.conf' file. Check the password you are providing, or check your Kerberos or ident software if the complaint mentions one of those authentication types.

```
FATAL:  user "andym" does not exist
```

The indicated user name was not found.

```
FATAL:  database "testdb" does not exist
```

The database you are trying to connect to does not exist. Note that if you do not specify a database name, it defaults to the database user name, which may or may not be the right thing.

Tip: The server log may contain more information about an authentication failure than is reported to the client. If you are confused about the reason for a failure, check the log.

---

[4] http://www.kernel.org/pub/linux/libs/pam/

[5] http://www.sun.com/software/solaris/pam/

8 Localization

This chapter describes the available localization features from the point of view of the administrator. PostgreSQL supports localization with two approaches:

- Using the locale features of the operating system to provide locale-specific collation order, number formatting, translated messages, and other aspects.

- Providing a number of different character sets defined in the PostgreSQL server, including multiple-byte character sets, to support storing text in all kinds of languages, and providing character set translation between client and server.

8.1 Locale Support

Locale support refers to an application respecting cultural preferences regarding alphabets, sorting, number formatting, etc. PostgreSQL uses the standard ISO C and POSIX locale facilities provided by the server operating system. For additional information refer to the documentation of your system.

8.1.1 Overview

Locale support is automatically initialized when a database cluster is created using initdb. initdb will initialize the database cluster with the locale setting of its execution environment by default, so if your system is already set to use the locale that you want in your database cluster then there is nothing else you need to do. If you want to use a different locale (or you are not sure which locale your system is set to), you can instruct initdb exactly which locale to use by specifying the --locale option. For example:

    initdb --locale=sv_SE

This example sets the locale to Swedish (sv) as spoken in Sweden (SE). Other possibilities might be en_US (U.S. English) and fr_CA (French Canadian). If more than one character set can be useful for a locale then the specifications look like this: cs_CZ.ISO8859-2. What locales are available under what names on your system depends on what was provided by the operating system vendor and what was installed. (On most systems, the command locale -a will provide a list of available locales.)

Occasionally it is useful to mix rules from several locales, e.g., use English collation rules but Spanish messages. To support that, a set of locale subcategories exist that control only a certain aspect of the localization rules:

LC_COLLATE	String sort order
LC_CTYPE	Character classification (What is a letter? Its upper-case equivalent?)
LC_MESSAGES	Language of messages
LC_MONETARY	Formatting of currency amounts
LC_NUMERIC	Formatting of numbers
LC_TIME	Formatting of dates and times

The category names translate into names of initdb options to override the locale choice for a specific category. For instance, to set the locale to French Canadian, but use U.S. rules for formatting currency, use initdb --locale=fr_CA --lc-monetary=en_US.

If you want the system to behave as if it had no locale support, use the special locale C or POSIX.

The nature of some locale categories is that their value has to be fixed for the lifetime of a database cluster. That is, once initdb has run, you cannot change them anymore. LC_COLLATE and LC_CTYPE are those categories. They affect the sort order of indexes, so they must be kept fixed, or indexes on text columns will become corrupt. PostgreSQL enforces this by recording the values of LC_COLLATE and LC_CTYPE that are seen by initdb. The server automatically adopts those two values when it is started.

The other locale categories can be changed as desired whenever the server is running by setting the run-time configuration variables that have the same name as the locale categories (see Section 4.10.2 *Locale and Formatting*, page 75 for details). The defaults that are chosen by initdb are actually only written into the configuration file 'postgresql.conf' to serve as defaults when the server is started. If you delete these assignments from 'postgresql.conf' then the server will inherit the settings from its execution environment.

Note that the locale behavior of the server is determined by the environment variables seen by the server, not by the environment of any client. Therefore, be careful to configure the correct locale settings before starting the server. A consequence of this is that if client and server are set up in different locales, messages may appear in different languages depending on where they originated.

> Note: When we speak of inheriting the locale from the execution environment, this means the following on most operating systems: For a given locale category, say the collation, the following environment variables are consulted in this order until one is found to be set: LC_ALL, LC_COLLATE (the variable corresponding to the respective category), LANG. If none of these environment variables are set then the locale defaults to C.
>
> Some message localization libraries also look at the environment variable LANGUAGE which overrides all other locale settings for the purpose of setting the language of messages. If in doubt, please refer to the documentation of your operating system, in particular the documentation about gettext, for more information.

To enable messages to be translated to the user's preferred language, NLS must have been enabled at build time. This choice is independent of the other locale support.

8.1.2 Behavior

The locale settings influence the following SQL features:

- Sort order in queries using ORDER BY on textual data
- The ability to use indexes with LIKE clauses
- The upper, lower, and initcap functions
- The to_char family of functions

The drawback of using locales other than C or POSIX in PostgreSQL is its performance impact. It slows character handling and prevents ordinary indexes from being used by LIKE. For this reason use locales only if you actually need them.

As a workaround to allow PostgreSQL to use indexes with LIKE clauses under a non-C locale, several custom operator classes exist. These allow the creation of an index that performs a strict character-by-character comparison, ignoring locale comparison rules. Refer to Volume 1, Section 9.8 *Operator Classes* for more information.

8.1.3 Problems

If locale support doesn't work in spite of the explanation above, check that the locale support in your operating system is correctly configured. To check what locales are installed on your system, you may use the command locale -a if your operating system provides it.

Check that PostgreSQL is actually using the locale that you think it is. LC_COLLATE and LC_CTYPE settings are determined at initdb time and cannot be changed without repeating initdb. Other locale settings including LC_MESSAGES and LC_MONETARY are initially determined by the environment the server is started in, but can be changed on-the-fly. You can check the active locale settings using the SHOW command.

The directory 'src/test/locale' in the source distribution contains a test suite for PostgreSQL's locale support.

Client applications that handle server-side errors by parsing the text of the error message will obviously have problems when the server's messages are in a different language. Authors of such applications are advised to make use of the error code scheme instead.

Maintaining catalogs of message translations requires the on-going efforts of many volunteers that want to see PostgreSQL speak their preferred language well. If messages in your language are currently not available or not fully translated, your assistance would be appreciated. If you want to help, refer to Volume 4, Chapter 5 *Native Language Support* or write to the developers' mailing list.

8.2 Character Set Support

The character set support in PostgreSQL allows you to store text in a variety of character sets, including single-byte character sets such as the ISO 8859 series and multiple-byte character sets such as EUC (Extended Unix Code), UTF-8, and Mule internal code. All supported character sets can be used transparently by clients, but a few are not supported for use within the server (that is, as a server-side encoding). The default character set is selected while initializing your PostgreSQL database cluster using initdb. It can be overridden when you create a database, so you can have multiple databases each with a different character set.

8.2.1 Supported Character Sets

Table 8.1 shows the character sets available for use in PostgreSQL.

Name	Description	Language	Server?	Bytes/Char	Aliases
BIG5	Big Five	Traditional Chinese	No	1-2	WIN950, Windows950
EUC_CN	Extended UNIX Code-CN	Simplified Chinese	Yes	1-3	
EUC_JP	Extended UNIX Code-JP	Japanese	Yes	1-3	
EUC_KR	Extended UNIX Code-KR	Korean	Yes	1-3	
EUC_TW	Extended UNIX Code-TW	Traditional Chinese, Taiwanese	Yes	1-3	
GB18030	National Standard	Chinese	No	1-2	
GBK	Extended National Standard	Simplified Chinese	No	1-2	WIN936, Windows936
ISO_8859_5	ISO 8859-5, ECMA 113	Latin/Cyrillic	Yes	1	
ISO_8859_6	ISO 8859-6, ECMA 114	Latin/Arabic	Yes	1	
ISO_8859_7	ISO 8859-7, ECMA 118	Latin/Greek	Yes	1	
ISO_8859_8	ISO 8859-8, ECMA 121	Latin/Hebrew	Yes	1	
JOHAB	JOHAB	Korean (Hangul)	Yes	1-3	
KOI8	KOI8-R(U)	Cyrillic	Yes	1	KOI8R
LATIN1	ISO 8859-1, ECMA 94	Western European	Yes	1	ISO88591

LATIN2	ISO 8859-2, ECMA 94	Central European	Yes	1	ISO88592
LATIN3	ISO 8859-3, ECMA 94	South European	Yes	1	ISO88593
LATIN4	ISO 8859-4, ECMA 94	North European	Yes	1	ISO88594
LATIN5	ISO 8859-9, ECMA 128	Turkish	Yes	1	ISO88599
LATIN6	ISO 8859-10, ECMA 144	Nordic	Yes	1	ISO885910
LATIN7	ISO 8859-13	Baltic	Yes	1	ISO885913
LATIN8	ISO 8859-14	Celtic	Yes	1	ISO885914
LATIN9	ISO 8859-15	LATIN1 with Euro and accents	Yes	1	ISO885915
LATIN10	ISO 8859-16, ASRO SR 14111	Romanian	Yes	1	ISO885916
MULE_INTERNAL	Mule internal code	Multilingual Emacs	Yes	1-4	
SJIS	Shift JIS	Japanese	No	1-2	Mskanji, ShiftJIS, WIN932, Windows932
SQL_ASCII	unspecified (see text)	*any*	Yes	1	
UHC	Unified Hangul Code	Korean	No	1-2	WIN949, Windows949
UTF8	Unicode, 8-bit	*all*	Yes	1-4	Unicode
WIN866	Windows CP866	Cyrillic	Yes	1	ALT
WIN874	Windows CP874	Thai	Yes	1	
WIN1250	Windows CP1250	Central European	Yes	1	
WIN1251	Windows CP1251	Cyrillic	Yes	1	WIN
WIN1252	Windows CP1252	Western European	Yes	1	
WIN1253	Windows CP1253	Greek	Yes	1	
WIN1254	Windows CP1254	Turkish	Yes	1	

WIN1255	Windows CP1255	Hebrew	Yes	1	
WIN1256	Windows CP1256	Arabic	Yes	1	
WIN1257	Windows CP1257	Baltic	Yes	1	
WIN1258	Windows CP1258	Vietnamese	Yes	1	ABC, TCVN, TCVN5712, VSCII

Table 8.1: PostgreSQL Character Sets

Not all APIs support all the listed character sets. For example, the Post-greSQL JDBC driver does not support MULE_INTERNAL, LATIN6, LATIN8, and LATIN10.

The SQL_ASCII setting behaves considerably differently from the other set-tings. When the server character set is SQL_ASCII, the server interprets byte values 0-127 according to the ASCII standard, while byte values 128-255 are taken as uninterpreted characters. No encoding conversion will be done when the setting is SQL_ASCII. Thus, this setting is not so much a declaration that a specific encoding is in use, as a declaration of ignorance about the encoding. In most cases, if you are working with any non-ASCII data, it is unwise to use the SQL_ASCII setting, because PostgreSQL will be unable to help you by converting or validating non-ASCII characters.

8.2.2 Setting the Character Set

initdb defines the default character set for a PostgreSQL cluster. For exam-ple,

    initdb -E EUC_JP

sets the default character set (encoding) to EUC_JP (Extended Unix Code for Japanese). You can use --encoding instead of -E if you prefer to type longer option strings. If no -E or --encoding option is given, initdb attempts to determine the appropriate encoding to use based on the specified or default locale.

You can create a database with a different character set:

    createdb -E EUC_KR korean

This will create a database named korean that uses the character set EUC_KR. Another way to accomplish this is to use this SQL command:

    CREATE DATABASE korean WITH ENCODING 'EUC_KR';

The encoding for a database is stored in the system catalog pg_database. You can see that by using the -l option or the \l command of psql.

```
$ psql -l
            List of databases
    Database   |  Owner  |   Encoding
---------------+---------+---------------
   euc_cn      | t-ishii | EUC_CN
   euc_jp      | t-ishii | EUC_JP
```

```
euc_kr          | t-ishii | EUC_KR
euc_tw          | t-ishii | EUC_TW
mule_internal   | t-ishii | MULE_INTERNAL
postgres        | t-ishii | EUC_JP
regression      | t-ishii | SQL_ASCII
template1       | t-ishii | EUC_JP
test            | t-ishii | EUC_JP
utf8            | t-ishii | UTF8
(9 rows)
```

Important: Although you can specify any encoding you want for a database, it is unwise to choose an encoding that is not what is expected by the locale you have selected. The LC_COLLATE and LC_CTYPE settings imply a particular encoding, and locale-dependent operations (such as sorting) are likely to misinterpret data that is in an incompatible encoding.

Since these locale settings are frozen by initdb, the apparent flexibility to use different encodings in different databases of a cluster is more theoretical than real. It is likely that these mechanisms will be revisited in future versions of PostgreSQL.

One way to use multiple encodings safely is to set the locale to C or POSIX during initdb, thus disabling any real locale awareness.

8.2.3 Automatic Character Set Conversion Between Server and Client

PostgreSQL supports automatic character set conversion between server and client for certain character set combinations. The conversion information is stored in the pg_conversion system catalog. PostgreSQL comes with some predefined conversions, as shown in Table 8.2. You can create a new conversion using the SQL command CREATE CONVERSION.

Server Character Set	Available Client Character Sets
BIG5	*not supported as a server encoding*
EUC_CN	*EUC_CN*, MULE_INTERNAL, UTF8
EUC_JP	*EUC_JP*, MULE_INTERNAL, SJIS, UTF8
EUC_KR	*EUC_KR*, MULE_INTERNAL, UTF8
EUC_TW	*EUC_TW*, BIG5, MULE_INTERNAL, UTF8
GB18030	*not supported as a server encoding*
GBK	*not supported as a server encoding*
ISO_8859_5	*ISO_8859_5*, KOI8, MULE_INTERNAL, UTF8, WIN866, WIN1251
ISO_8859_6	*ISO_8859_6*, UTF8
ISO_8859_7	*ISO_8859_7*, UTF8
ISO_8859_8	*ISO_8859_8*, UTF8
JOHAB	*JOHAB*, UTF8
KOI8	*KOI8*, ISO_8859_5, MULE_INTERNAL, UTF8, WIN866, WIN1251
LATIN1	*LATIN1*, MULE_INTERNAL, UTF8
LATIN2	*LATIN2*, MULE_INTERNAL, UTF8, WIN1250
LATIN3	*LATIN3*, MULE_INTERNAL, UTF8
LATIN4	*LATIN4*, MULE_INTERNAL, UTF8
LATIN5	*LATIN5*, UTF8
LATIN6	*LATIN6*, UTF8
LATIN7	*LATIN7*, UTF8
LATIN8	*LATIN8*, UTF8
LATIN9	*LATIN9*, UTF8
LATIN10	*LATIN10*, UTF8
MULE_INTERNAL	*MULE_INTERNAL*, BIG5, EUC_CN, EUC_JP, EUC_KR, EUC_TW, ISO_8859_5, KOI8, LATIN1 to LATIN4, SJIS, WIN866, WIN1250, WIN1251
SJIS	*not supported as a server encoding*
SQL_ASCII	*any (no conversion will be performed)*
UHC	*not supported as a server encoding*
UTF8	*all supported encodings*
WIN866	*WIN866*, ISO_8859_5, KOI8, MULE_INTERNAL, UTF8, WIN1251
WIN874	*WIN874*, UTF8
WIN1250	*WIN1250*, LATIN2, MULE_INTERNAL, UTF8
WIN1251	*WIN1251*, ISO_8859_5, KOI8, MULE_INTERNAL, UTF8, WIN866
WIN1252	*WIN1252*, UTF8
WIN1253	*WIN1253*, UTF8
WIN1254	*WIN1254*, UTF8
WIN1255	*WIN1255*, UTF8
WIN1256	*WIN1256*, UTF8
WIN1257	*WIN1257*, UTF8
WIN1258	*WIN1258*, UTF8

Table 8.2: Client/Server Character Set Conversions

To enable automatic character set conversion, you have to tell PostgreSQL
the character set (encoding) you would like to use in the client. There are
several ways to accomplish this:

- Using the \encoding command in psql. \encoding allows you to change
  client encoding on the fly. For example, to change the encoding to SJIS,
  type:

  \encoding SJIS

- Using libpq functions. \encoding actually calls PQsetClientEncoding()
  for its purpose.

  int PQsetClientEncoding(PGconn *conn, const char *encoding);

  where conn is a connection to the server, and encoding is the encoding you
  want to use. If the function successfully sets the encoding, it returns 0,
  otherwise -1. The current encoding for this connection can be determined
  by using:

  int PQclientEncoding(const PGconn *conn);

  Note that it returns the encoding ID, not a symbolic string such as EUC_JP.
  To convert an encoding ID to an encoding name, you can use:

  char *pg_encoding_to_char(int encoding_id);

- Using SET client_encoding TO. Setting the client encoding can be done
  with this SQL command:

  SET CLIENT_ENCODING TO 'value';

  Also you can use the standard SQL syntax SET NAMES for this purpose:

  SET NAMES 'value';

  To query the current client encoding:

  SHOW client_encoding;

  To return to the default encoding:

  RESET client_encoding;

- Using PGCLIENTENCODING. If the environment variable PGCLIENTENCODING
  is defined in the client's environment, that client encoding is automatically
  selected when a connection to the server is made. (This can subsequently
  be overridden using any of the other methods mentioned above.)

- Using the configuration variable client_encoding. If the client_
  encoding variable is set, that client encoding is automatically selected
  when a connection to the server is made. (This can subsequently be
  overridden using any of the other methods mentioned above.)

If the conversion of a particular character is not possible—suppose you chose
EUC_JP for the server and LATIN1 for the client, then some Japanese characters
do not have a representation in LATIN1—then an error is reported.

If the client character set is defined as SQL_ASCII, encoding conversion is
disabled, regardless of the server's character set. Just as for the server, use of
SQL_ASCII is unwise unless you are working with all-ASCII data.

8.2.4 Further Reading

These are good sources to start learning about various kinds of encoding systems.

`http://www.i18ngurus.com/`
> An extensive collection of documents about character sets, encodings, and code pages.

`ftp://ftp.ora.com/pub/examples/nutshell/ujip/doc/cjk.inf`
> Detailed explanations of EUC_JP, EUC_CN, EUC_KR, EUC_TW appear in section 3.2.

`http://www.unicode.org/`
> The web site of the Unicode Consortium

RFC 2044
> UTF-8 is defined here.

9 Routine Database Maintenance Tasks

PostgreSQL, like any database software, requires that certain tasks be performed regularly to achieve optimum performance. The tasks discussed here are *required*, but they are repetitive in nature and can easily be automated using standard Unix tools such as cron scripts or Windows' Task Scheduler. But it is the database administrator's responsibility to set up appropriate scripts, and to check that they execute successfully.

One obvious maintenance task is creation of backup copies of the data on a regular schedule. Without a recent backup, you have no chance of recovery after a catastrophe (disk failure, fire, mistakenly dropping a critical table, etc.). The backup and recovery mechanisms available in PostgreSQL are discussed at length in Chapter 10 *Backup and Restore*, page 131.

The other main category of maintenance task is periodic "vacuuming" of the database. This activity is discussed in Section 9.1 *Routine Vacuuming*. Closely related to this is updating the statistics that will be used by the query planner, as discussed in Section 9.1.2 *Updating planner statistics*, page 123.

Another task that might need periodic attention is log file management. This is discussed in Section 9.3 *Log File Maintenance*, page 128.

PostgreSQL is low-maintenance compared to some other database management systems. Nonetheless, appropriate attention to these tasks will go far towards ensuring a pleasant and productive experience with the system.

9.1 Routine Vacuuming

PostgreSQL's VACUUM command *must* be run on a regular basis for several reasons:

1. To recover or reuse disk space occupied by updated or deleted rows.

2. To update data statistics used by the PostgreSQL query planner.

3. To protect against loss of very old data due to *transaction ID wraparound*.

The frequency and scope of the VACUUM operations performed for each of these reasons will vary depending on the needs of each site. Therefore, database administrators must understand these issues and develop an appropriate maintenance strategy. This section concentrates on explaining the high-level issues; for details about command syntax and so on, see the VACUUM reference page.

The standard form of VACUUM can run in parallel with production database operations. Commands such as SELECT, INSERT, UPDATE, and DELETE will continue to function as normal, though you will not be able to modify the definition of a table with commands such as ALTER TABLE ADD COLUMN while it is being vacuumed. Also, VACUUM requires a substantial amount of I/O traffic, which can cause poor performance for other active sessions. There are configuration parameters that can be adjusted to reduce the performance impact of background vacuuming—see Section 4.4.4 *Cost-Based Vacuum Delay* , page 54.

An automated mechanism for performing the necessary VACUUM operations has been added in PostgreSQL 8.1. See Section 9.1.4 *The auto-vacuum daemon*, page 126.

9.1.1 Recovering disk space

In normal PostgreSQL operation, an UPDATE or DELETE of a row does not immediately remove the old version of the row. This approach is necessary to gain the benefits of multiversion concurrency control (see Volume 1, Chapter 10 *Concurrency Control*): the row version must not be deleted while it is still potentially visible to other transactions. But eventually, an outdated or deleted row version is no longer of interest to any transaction. The space it occupies must be reclaimed for reuse by new rows, to avoid infinite growth of disk space requirements. This is done by running VACUUM.

Clearly, a table that receives frequent updates or deletes will need to be vacuumed more often than tables that are seldom updated. It may be useful to set up periodic cron tasks that VACUUM only selected tables, skipping tables that are known not to change often. This is only likely to be helpful if you have both large heavily-updated tables and large seldom-updated tables—the extra cost of vacuuming a small table isn't enough to be worth worrying about.

There are two variants of the VACUUM command. The first form, known as "lazy vacuum" or just VACUUM, marks expired data in tables and indexes for future reuse; it does *not* attempt to reclaim the space used by this expired data unless the space is at the end of the table and an exclusive table lock can be easily obtained. Unused space at the start or middle of the file does not result in the file being shortened and space returned to the operating system. This variant of VACUUM can be run concurrently with normal database operations.

The second form is the VACUUM FULL command. This uses a more aggressive algorithm for reclaiming the space consumed by expired row versions. Any space that is freed by VACUUM FULL is immediately returned to the operating system. Unfortunately, this variant of the VACUUM command acquires an exclusive lock on each table while VACUUM FULL is processing it. Therefore, frequently using VACUUM FULL can have an extremely negative effect on the performance of concurrent database queries.

The standard form of VACUUM is best used with the goal of maintaining a fairly level steady-state usage of disk space. If you need to return disk space to the operating system you can use VACUUM FULL—but what's the point of releasing disk space that will only have to be allocated again soon? Moderately frequent standard VACUUM runs are a better approach than infrequent VACUUM FULL runs for maintaining heavily-updated tables.

Recommended practice for most sites is to schedule a database-wide VACUUM once a day at a low-usage time of day, supplemented by more frequent vacuuming of heavily-updated tables if necessary. (Some installations with extremely high update rates vacuum their busiest tables as often as once every few minutes.) If you have multiple databases in a cluster, don't forget to VACUUM each one; the program vacuumdb may be helpful.

VACUUM FULL is recommended for cases where you know you have deleted the majority of rows in a table, so that the steady-state size of the table can be shrunk substantially with VACUUM FULL's more aggressive approach. Use plain VACUUM, not VACUUM FULL, for routine vacuuming for space recovery.

If you have a table whose entire contents are deleted on a periodic basis, consider doing it with TRUNCATE rather than using DELETE followed by VACUUM. TRUNCATE removes the entire content of the table immediately, without requiring a subsequent VACUUM or VACUUM FULL to reclaim the now-unused disk space.

9.1.2 Updating planner statistics

The PostgreSQL query planner relies on statistical information about the contents of tables in order to generate good plans for queries. These statistics are gathered by the ANALYZE command, which can be invoked by itself or as an optional step in VACUUM. It is important to have reasonably accurate statistics, otherwise poor choices of plans may degrade database performance.

As with vacuuming for space recovery, frequent updates of statistics are more useful for heavily-updated tables than for seldom-updated ones. But even for a heavily-updated table, there may be no need for statistics updates if the statistical distribution of the data is not changing much. A simple rule of thumb is to think about how much the minimum and maximum values of the columns in the table change. For example, a timestamp column that contains the time of row update will have a constantly-increasing maximum value as rows are added and updated; such a column will probably need more frequent statistics updates than, say, a column containing URLs for pages accessed on a website. The URL column may receive changes just as often, but the statistical distribution of its values probably changes relatively slowly.

It is possible to run ANALYZE on specific tables and even just specific columns of a table, so the flexibility exists to update some statistics more frequently than others if your application requires it. In practice, however, it is usually best to just analyze the entire database because it is a fast operation. It uses a statistical random sampling of the rows of a table rather than reading every single row.

> **Tip:** Although per-column tweaking of ANALYZE frequency may not be very productive, you may well find it worthwhile to do per-column adjustment of the level of detail of the statistics collected by ANALYZE. Columns that are heavily used in WHERE clauses and have highly irregular data distributions may require a finer-grain data histogram than other columns. See ALTER TABLE SET STATISTICS.

Recommended practice for most sites is to schedule a database-wide ANALYZE once a day at a low-usage time of day; this can usefully be combined with a nightly VACUUM. However, sites with relatively slowly changing table statistics may find that this is overkill, and that less-frequent ANALYZE runs are sufficient.

9.1.3 Preventing transaction ID wraparound failures

PostgreSQL's MVCC transaction semantics depend on being able to compare transaction ID (XID) numbers: a row version with an insertion XID greater than the current transaction's XID is "in the future" and should not be visible to the current transaction. But since transaction IDs have limited size (32 bits at this writing) a cluster that runs for a long time (more than 4 billion transactions) would suffer *transaction ID wraparound*: the XID counter wraps around to zero, and all of a sudden transactions that were in the past appear to be in the future—which means their outputs become invisible. In short, catastrophic data loss. (Actually the data is still there, but that's cold comfort if you can't get at it.) To avoid this, it is necessary to vacuum every table in every database at least once every two billion transactions.

The reason that periodic vacuuming solves the problem is that PostgreSQL distinguishes a special XID FrozenXID. This XID is always considered older than every normal XID. Normal XIDs are compared using modulo-2^{31} arithmetic. This means that for every normal XID, there are two billion XIDs that are "older" and two billion that are "newer"; another way to say it is that the normal XID space is circular with no endpoint. Therefore, once a row version has been created with a particular normal XID, the row version will appear to be "in the past" for the next two billion transactions, no matter which normal XID we are talking about. If the row version still exists after more than two billion transactions, it will suddenly appear to be in the future. To prevent data loss, old row versions must be reassigned the XID FrozenXID sometime before they reach the two-billion-transactions-old mark. Once they are assigned this special XID, they will appear to be "in the past" to all normal transactions regardless of wraparound issues, and so such row versions will be good until deleted, no matter how long that is. This reassignment of old XIDs is handled by VACUUM.

VACUUM's behavior is controlled by the configuration parameter vacuum_freeze_min_age: any XID older than vacuum_freeze_min_age transactions is replaced by FrozenXID. Larger values of vacuum_freeze_min_age preserve transactional information longer, while smaller values increase the number of transactions that can elapse before the table must be vacuumed again.

The maximum time that a table can go unvacuumed is two billion transactions minus the vacuum_freeze_min_age that was used when it was last vacuumed. If it were to go unvacuumed for longer than that, data loss could result. To ensure that this does not happen, the *autovacuum* facility described in Section 9.1.4 *The auto-vacuum daemon*, page 126 is invoked on any table that might contain XIDs older than the age specified by the configuration parameter autovacuum_freeze_max_age. (This will happen even if autovacuum is otherwise disabled.)

This implies that if a table is not otherwise vacuumed, autovacuum will be invoked on it approximately once every autovacuum_freeze_max_age minus vacuum_freeze_min_age transactions. For tables that are regularly vacuumed for space reclamation purposes, this is of little importance. However, for static tables (including tables that receive inserts, but no updates or deletes), there is no need for vacuuming for space reclamation, and so it can be useful to try to maximize the interval between forced autovacuums on very large static tables.

Obviously one can do this either by increasing `autovacuum_freeze_max_age` or by decreasing `vacuum_freeze_min_age`.

The sole disadvantage of increasing `autovacuum_freeze_max_age` is that the 'pg_clog' subdirectory of the database cluster will take more space, because it must store the commit status for all transactions back to the `autovacuum_freeze_max_age` horizon. The commit status uses two bits per transaction, so if `autovacuum_freeze_max_age` has its maximum allowed value of a little less than two billion, 'pg_clog' can be expected to grow to about half a gigabyte. If this is trivial compared to your total database size, setting `autovacuum_freeze_max_age` to its maximum allowed value is recommended. Otherwise, set it depending on what you are willing to allow for 'pg_clog' storage. (The default, 200 million transactions, translates to about 50MB of 'pg_clog' storage.)

One disadvantage of decreasing `vacuum_freeze_min_age` is that it may cause VACUUM to do useless work: changing a table row's XID to FrozenXID is a waste of time if the row is modified soon thereafter (causing it to acquire a new XID). So the setting should be large enough that rows are not frozen until they are unlikely to change any more. Another disadvantage of decreasing this setting is that details about exactly which transaction inserted or modified a row will be lost sooner. This information sometimes comes in handy, particularly when trying to analyze what went wrong after a database failure. For these two reasons, decreasing this setting is not recommended except for completely static tables.

To track the age of the oldest XIDs in a database, VACUUM stores XID statistics in the system tables `pg_class` and `pg_database`. In particular, the `relfrozenxid` column of a table's `pg_class` row contains the freeze cutoff XID that was used by the last VACUUM for that table. All normal XIDs older than this cutoff XID are guaranteed to have been replaced by FrozenXID within the table. Similarly, the `datfrozenxid` column of a database's `pg_database` row is a lower bound on the normal XIDs appearing in that database—it is just the minimum of the per-table `relfrozenxid` values within the database. A convenient way to examine this information is to execute queries such as

```
SELECT relname, age(relfrozenxid) FROM pg_class WHERE relkind
= 'r';
SELECT datname, age(datfrozenxid) FROM pg_database;
```

The age column measures the number of transactions from the cutoff XID to the current transaction's XID. Immediately after a VACUUM, `age(relfrozenxid)` should be a little more than the `vacuum_freeze_min_age` setting that was used (more by the number of transactions started since the VACUUM started). If `age(relfrozenxid)` exceeds `autovacuum_freeze_max_age`, an autovacuum will soon be forced for the table.

If for some reason autovacuum fails to clear old XIDs from a table, the system will begin to emit warning messages like this when the database's oldest XIDs reach ten million transactions from the wraparound point:

```
WARNING:  database "mydb" must be vacuumed within 177009986
 transactions
HINT:  To avoid a database shutdown, execute a full-database
 VACUUM in "mydb".
```

If these warnings are ignored, the system will shut down and refuse to execute any new transactions once there are fewer than 1 million transactions left until wraparound:

```
ERROR:  database is shut down to avoid wraparound data loss
 in database "mydb"
HINT:  Stop the postmaster and use a standalone backend to
 VACUUM in "mydb".
```

The 1-million-transaction safety margin exists to let the administrator recover without data loss, by manually executing the required VACUUM commands. However, since the system will not execute commands once it has gone into the safety shutdown mode, the only way to do this is to stop the server and use a single-user backend to execute VACUUM. The shutdown mode is not enforced by a single-user backend. See the postgres reference page for details about using a single-user backend.

9.1.4 The auto-vacuum daemon

Beginning in PostgreSQL 8.1, there is a separate optional server process called the *autovacuum daemon*, whose purpose is to automate the execution of VACUUM and ANALYZE commands. When enabled, the autovacuum daemon runs periodically and checks for tables that have had a large number of inserted, updated or deleted tuples. These checks use the row-level statistics collection facility; therefore, the autovacuum daemon cannot be used unless stats_start_collector and stats_row_level are set to true. Also, it's important to allow a slot for the autovacuum process when choosing the value of superuser_reserved_connections.

The autovacuum daemon, when enabled, runs every autovacuum_naptime seconds. On each run, it selects one database to process and checks each table within that database. VACUUM or ANALYZE commands are issued as needed.

Tables whose relfrozenxid value is more than autovacuum_freeze_max_age transactions old are always vacuumed. Otherwise, two conditions are used to determine which operation(s) to apply. If the number of obsolete tuples since the last VACUUM exceeds the "vacuum threshold", the table is vacuumed. The vacuum threshold is defined as:

```
vacuum threshold = vacuum base threshold + vacuum scale
 factor * number of tuples
```

where the vacuum base threshold is autovacuum_vacuum_threshold, the vacuum scale factor is autovacuum_vacuum_scale_factor, and the number of tuples is pg_class.reltuples. The number of obsolete tuples is obtained from the statistics collector; it is a semi-accurate count updated by each UPDATE and DELETE operation. (It is only semi-accurate because some information may be lost under heavy load.) For analyze, a similar condition is used: the threshold, defined as

```
analyze threshold = analyze base threshold + analyze scale
    factor * number of tuples
```

is compared to the total number of tuples inserted, updated, or deleted since
the last ANALYZE.

The default thresholds and scale factors are taken from 'postgresql.conf',
but it is possible to override them on a table-by-table basis by making entries in
the system catalog pg_autovacuum (Volume 4). If a pg_autovacuum row exists
for a particular table, the settings it specifies are applied; otherwise the global
settings are used. See Section 4.9 *Automatic Vacuuming*, page 71 for more
details on the global settings.

Besides the base threshold values and scale factors, there are five more parameters that can be set for each table in pg_autovacuum. The first, pg_
autovacuum.enabled, can be set to false to instruct the autovacuum daemon to
skip that particular table entirely. In this case autovacuum will only touch the
table if it must do so to prevent transaction ID wraparound. The next two parameters, the vacuum cost delay (pg_autovacuum.vac_cost_delay) and the vacuum cost limit (pg_autovacuum.vac_cost_limit), are used to set table-specific
values for the Cost-Based Vacuum Delay feature. The last two parameters,
(pg_autovacuum.freeze_min_age) and (pg_autovacuum.freeze_max_age), are
used to set table-specific values for vacuum_freeze_min_age and autovacuum_
freeze_max_age respectively.

If any of the values in pg_autovacuum are set to a negative number, or if a row
is not present at all in pg_autovacuum for any particular table, the corresponding
values from 'postgresql.conf' are used.

There is not currently any support for making pg_autovacuum entries, except
by doing manual INSERTs into the catalog. This feature will be improved in
future releases, and it is likely that the catalog definition will change.

> **Caution:** The contents of the pg_autovacuum system catalog are
> currently not saved in database dumps created by the tools pg_dump
> and pg_dumpall. If you want to preserve them across a dump/reload
> cycle, make sure you dump the catalog manually.

9.2 Routine Reindexing

In some situations it is worthwhile to rebuild indexes periodically with the
REINDEX command.

In PostgreSQL releases before 7.4, periodic reindexing was frequently necessary to avoid "index bloat", due to lack of internal space reclamation in B-tree
indexes. Any situation in which the range of index keys changed over time—for
example, an index on timestamps in a table where old entries are eventually
deleted—would result in bloat, because index pages for no-longer-needed por-
tions of the key range were not reclaimed for re-use. Over time, the index size
could become indefinitely much larger than the amount of useful data in it.

In PostgreSQL 7.4 and later, index pages that have become completely empty
are reclaimed for re-use. There is still a possibility for inefficient use of space:
if all but a few index keys on a page have been deleted, the page remains
allocated. So a usage pattern in which all but a few keys in each range are

eventually deleted will see poor use of space. For such usage patterns, periodic reindexing is recommended.

The potential for bloat in non-B-tree indexes has not been well characterized. It is a good idea to keep an eye on the index's physical size when using any non-B-tree index type.

Also, for B-tree indexes a freshly-constructed index is somewhat faster to access than one that has been updated many times, because logically adjacent pages are usually also physically adjacent in a newly built index. (This consideration does not currently apply to non-B-tree indexes.) It might be worthwhile to reindex periodically just to improve access speed.

9.3 Log File Maintenance

It is a good idea to save the database server's log output somewhere, rather than just routing it to '/dev/null'. The log output is invaluable when it comes time to diagnose problems. However, the log output tends to be voluminous (especially at higher debug levels) and you won't want to save it indefinitely. You need to "rotate" the log files so that new log files are started and old ones removed after a reasonable period of time.

If you simply direct the stderr of postgres into a file, you will have log output, but the only way to truncate the log file is to stop and restart the server. This may be OK if you are using PostgreSQL in a development environment, but few production servers would find this behavior acceptable.

A better approach is to send the server's stderr output to some type of log rotation program. There is a built-in log rotation program, which you can use by setting the configuration parameter redirect_stderr to true in 'postgresql.conf'. The control parameters for this program are described in Section 4.7.1 *Where To Log*, page 64.

Alternatively, you might prefer to use an external log rotation program, if you have one that you are already using with other server software. For example, the rotatelogs tool included in the Apache distribution can be used with PostgreSQL. To do this, just pipe the server's stderr output to the desired program. If you start the server with pg_ctl, then stderr is already redirected to stdout, so you just need a pipe command, for example:

```
pg_ctl start | rotatelogs /var/log/pgsql_log 86400
```

Another production-grade approach to managing log output is to send it all to syslog and let syslog deal with file rotation. To do this, set the configuration parameter log_destination to syslog (to log to syslog only) in 'postgresql.conf'. Then you can send a SIGHUP signal to the syslog daemon whenever you want to force it to start writing a new log file. If you want to automate log rotation, the logrotate program can be configured to work with log files from syslog.

On many systems, however, syslog is not very reliable, particularly with large log messages; it may truncate or drop messages just when you need them the most. Also, on Linux, syslog will sync each message to disk, yielding poor performance. (You can use a - at the start of the file name in the syslog configuration file to disable this behavior.)

Note that all the solutions described above take care of starting new log files at configurable intervals, but they do not handle deletion of old, no-longer-interesting log files. You will probably want to set up a batch job to periodically delete old log files. Another possibility is to configure the rotation program so that old log files are overwritten cyclically.

10 Backup and Restore

As with everything that contains valuable data, PostgreSQL databases should be backed up regularly. While the procedure is essentially simple, it is important to have a basic understanding of the underlying techniques and assumptions.

There are three fundamentally different approaches to backing up PostgreSQL data:

- SQL dump
- File system level backup
- Continuous archiving

Each has its own strengths and weaknesses.

10.1 SQL Dump

The idea behind this dump method is to generate a text file with SQL commands that, when fed back to the server, will recreate the database in the same state as it was at the time of the dump. PostgreSQL provides the utility program pg_dump for this purpose. The basic usage of this command is:

```
pg_dump dbname > outfile
```

As you see, pg_dump writes its results to the standard output. We will see below how this can be useful.

pg_dump is a regular PostgreSQL client application (albeit a particularly clever one). This means that you can do this backup procedure from any remote host that has access to the database. But remember that pg_dump does not operate with special permissions. In particular, it must have read access to all tables that you want to back up, so in practice you almost always have to run it as a database superuser.

To specify which database server pg_dump should contact, use the command line options -h *host* and -p *port*. The default host is the local host or whatever your PGHOST environment variable specifies. Similarly, the default port is indicated by the PGPORT environment variable or, failing that, by the compiled-in default. (Conveniently, the server will normally have the same compiled-in default.)

As any other PostgreSQL client application, pg_dump will by default connect with the database user name that is equal to the current operating system user name. To override this, either specify the -U option or set the environment variable PGUSER. Remember that pg_dump connections are subject to the normal client authentication mechanisms (which are described in Chapter 7 *Client Authentication*, page 99).

Dumps created by pg_dump are internally consistent, that is, updates to the database while pg_dump is running will not be in the dump. pg_dump does not block other operations on the database while it is working. (Exceptions are those operations that need to operate with an exclusive lock, such as VACUUM FULL.)

Important: If your database schema relies on OIDs (for instance as foreign keys) you must instruct pg_dump to dump the OIDs as well. To do this, use the -o command line option.

10.1.1 Restoring the dump

The text files created by pg_dump are intended to be read in by the psql program. The general command form to restore a dump is

    psql dbname < infile

where *infile* is what you used as *outfile* for the pg_dump command. The database *dbname* will not be created by this command, so you must create it yourself from template0 before executing psql (e.g., with createdb -T template0 db-name). psql supports similar options to pg_dump for specifying the database server to connect to and the user name to use. See the psql reference page for more information.

Before restoring a SQL dump, all the users who own objects or were granted permissions on objects in the dumped database must already exist. If they do not, then the restore will fail to recreate the objects with the original ownership and/or permissions. (Sometimes this is what you want, but usually it is not.)

By default, the psql script will continue to execute after an SQL error is encountered. You may wish to use the following command at the top of the script to alter that behaviour and have psql exit with an exit status of 3 if an SQL error occurs:

    \set ON_ERROR_STOP

Either way, you will only have a partially restored dump. Alternatively, you can specify that the whole dump should be restored as a single transaction, so the restore is either fully completed or fully rolled back. This mode can be specified by passing the -1 or --single-transaction command-line options to psql. When using this mode, be aware that even the smallest of errors can rollback a restore that has already run for many hours. However, that may still be preferable to manually cleaning up a complex database after a partially restored dump.

The ability of pg_dump and psql to write to or read from pipes makes it possible to dump a database directly from one server to another; for example:

    pg_dump -h host1 dbname | psql -h host2 dbname

Important: The dumps produced by pg_dump are relative to template0. This means that any languages, procedures, etc. added to template1 will also be dumped by pg_dump. As a result, when restoring, if you are using a customized template1, you must create the empty database from template0, as in the example above.

After restoring a backup, it is wise to run ANALYZE on each database so the query optimizer has useful statistics. An easy way to do this is to run vacuumdb -a -z; this is equivalent to running VACUUM ANALYZE on each database manually. For more advice on how to load large amounts of data into PostgreSQL efficiently, refer to Volume 1, Section 11.4 *Populating a Database*.

10.1.2 Using pg_dumpall

pg_dump dumps only a single database at a time, and it does not dump information about roles or tablespaces (because those are cluster-wide rather than per-database). To support convenient dumping of the entire contents of a database cluster, the pg_dumpall program is provided. pg_dumpall backs up each database in a given cluster, and also preserves cluster-wide data such as role and tablespace definitions. The basic usage of this command is:

```
pg_dumpall > outfile
```

The resulting dump can be restored with psql:

```
psql -f infile postgres
```

(Actually, you can specify any existing database name to start from, but if you are reloading in an empty cluster then postgres should generally be used.) It is always necessary to have database superuser access when restoring a pg_dumpall dump, as that is required to restore the role and tablespace information. If you use tablespaces, be careful that the tablespace paths in the dump are appropriate for the new installation.

10.1.3 Handling large databases

Since PostgreSQL allows tables larger than the maximum file size on your system, it can be problematic to dump such a table to a file, since the resulting file will likely be larger than the maximum size allowed by your system. Since pg_dump can write to the standard output, you can use standard Unix tools to work around this possible problem.

Use compressed dumps..   You can use your favorite compression program, for example gzip.

```
pg_dump dbname | gzip > filename.gz
```

Reload with

```
createdb dbname
gunzip -c filename.gz | psql dbname
```

or

```
cat filename.gz | gunzip | psql dbname
```

Use split.. The split command allows you to split the output into pieces that are acceptable in size to the underlying file system. For example, to make chunks of 1 megabyte:

```
pg_dump dbname | split -b 1m - filename
```

Reload with

```
createdb dbname
cat filename* | psql dbname
```

Use the custom dump format..   If PostgreSQL was built on a system with the zlib compression library installed, the custom dump format will compress data as it writes it to the output file. This will produce dump file sizes similar to using gzip, but it has the added advantage that tables can be restored selectively. The following command dumps a database using the custom dump format:

```
pg_dump -Fc dbname > filename
```
A custom-format dump is not a script for psql, but instead must be restored
with pg_restore. See the pg_dump and pg_restore reference pages for details.

10.2 File System Level Backup

An alternative backup strategy is to directly copy the files that PostgreSQL
uses to store the data in the database. In Section 3.2 *Creating a Database
Cluster*, page 27 it is explained where these files are located, but you have
probably found them already if you are interested in this method. You can use
whatever method you prefer for doing usual file system backups, for example

```
tar -cf backup.tar /usr/local/pgsql/data
```
There are two restrictions, however, which make this method impractical, or
at least inferior to the pg_dump method:

1. The database server *must* be shut down in order to get a usable backup.
   Half-way measures such as disallowing all connections will *not* work
   (mainly because tar and similar tools do not take an atomic snapshot
   of the state of the file system at a point in time). Information about stopping the server can be found in Section 3.5 *Shutting Down the Server*,
   page 40. Needless to say that you also need to shut down the server before
   restoring the data.

2. If you have dug into the details of the file system layout of the database,
   you may be tempted to try to back up or restore only certain individual
   tables or databases from their respective files or directories. This will *not*
   work because the information contained in these files contains only half the
   truth. The other half is in the commit log files 'pg_clog/*', which contain
   the commit status of all transactions. A table file is only usable with this
   information. Of course it is also impossible to restore only a table and the
   associated 'pg_clog' data because that would render all other tables in the
   database cluster useless. So file system backups only work for complete
   restoration of an entire database cluster.

An alternative file-system backup approach is to make a "consistent snapshot" of the data directory, if the file system supports that functionality (and
you are willing to trust that it is implemented correctly). The typical procedure is to make a "frozen snapshot" of the volume containing the database, then
copy the whole data directory (not just parts, see above) from the snapshot to
a backup device, then release the frozen snapshot. This will work even while
the database server is running. However, a backup created in this way saves the
database files in a state where the database server was not properly shut down;
therefore, when you start the database server on the backed-up data, it will
think the server had crashed and replay the WAL log. This is not a problem,
just be aware of it (and be sure to include the WAL files in your backup).

If your database is spread across multiple file systems, there may not be any
way to obtain exactly-simultaneous frozen snapshots of all the volumes. For
example, if your data files and WAL log are on different disks, or if tablespaces
are on different file systems, it might not be possible to use snapshot backup

because the snapshots must be simultaneous. Read your file system documentation very carefully before trusting to the consistent-snapshot technique in such
situations. The safest approach is to shut down the database server for long
enough to establish all the frozen snapshots.

Another option is to use rsync to perform a file system backup. This is done
by first running rsync while the database server is running, then shutting down
the database server just long enough to do a second rsync. The second rsync will
be much quicker than the first, because it has relatively little data to transfer,
and the end result will be consistent because the server was down. This method
allows a file system backup to be performed with minimal downtime.

Note that a file system backup will not necessarily be smaller than an SQL
dump. On the contrary, it will most likely be larger. (pg_dump does not need
to dump the contents of indexes for example, just the commands to recreate
them.)

10.3 Continuous Archiving and Point-In-Time Recovery (PITR)

At all times, PostgreSQL maintains a *write ahead log* (WAL) in the
'pg_xlog/' subdirectory of the cluster's data directory. The log describes every
change made to the database's data files. This log exists primarily for crash-
safety purposes: if the system crashes, the database can be restored to consistency by "replaying" the log entries made since the last checkpoint. However,
the existence of the log makes it possible to use a third strategy for backing up
databases: we can combine a file-system-level backup with backup of the WAL
files. If recovery is needed, we restore the backup and then replay from the
backed-up WAL files to bring the backup up to current time. This approach is
more complex to administer than either of the previous approaches, but it has
some significant benefits:

- We do not need a perfectly consistent backup as the starting point. Any
  internal inconsistency in the backup will be corrected by log replay (this is
  not significantly different from what happens during crash recovery). So
  we don't need file system snapshot capability, just tar or a similar archiving
  tool.

- Since we can string together an indefinitely long sequence of WAL files for
  replay, continuous backup can be achieved simply by continuing to archive
  the WAL files. This is particularly valuable for large databases, where it
  may not be convenient to take a full backup frequently.

- There is nothing that says we have to replay the WAL entries all the way
  to the end. We could stop the replay at any point and have a consistent
  snapshot of the database as it was at that time. Thus, this technique
  supports *point-in-time recovery*: it is possible to restore the database to
  its state at any time since your base backup was taken.

- If we continuously feed the series of WAL files to another machine that
  has been loaded with the same base backup file, we have a *warm standby*
  system: at any point we can bring up the second machine and it will have
  a nearly-current copy of the database.

As with the plain file-system-backup technique, this method can only support restoration of an entire database cluster, not a subset. Also, it requires a lot of archival storage: the base backup may be bulky, and a busy system will generate many megabytes of WAL traffic that have to be archived. Still, it is the preferred backup technique in many situations where high reliability is needed.

To recover successfully using continuous archiving (also called "online backup" by many database vendors), you need a continuous sequence of archived WAL files that extends back at least as far as the start time of your backup. So to get started, you should setup and test your procedure for archiving WAL files *before* you take your first base backup. Accordingly, we first discuss the mechanics of archiving WAL files.

10.3.1 Setting up WAL archiving

In an abstract sense, a running PostgreSQL system produces an indefinitely long sequence of WAL records. The system physically divides this sequence into WAL *segment files*, which are normally 16MB apiece (although the size can be altered when building PostgreSQL). The segment files are given numeric names that reflect their position in the abstract WAL sequence. When not using WAL archiving, the system normally creates just a few segment files and then "recycles" them by renaming no-longer-needed segment files to higher segment numbers. It's assumed that a segment file whose contents precede the checkpoint-before-last is no longer of interest and can be recycled.

When archiving WAL data, we want to capture the contents of each segment file once it is filled, and save that data somewhere before the segment file is recycled for reuse. Depending on the application and the available hardware, there could be many different ways of "saving the data somewhere": we could copy the segment files to an NFS-mounted directory on another machine, write them onto a tape drive (ensuring that you have a way of identifying the original name of each file), or batch them together and burn them onto CDs, or something else entirely. To provide the database administrator with as much flexibility as possible, PostgreSQL tries not to make any assumptions about how the archiving will be done. Instead, PostgreSQL lets the administrator specify a shell command to be executed to copy a completed segment file to wherever it needs to go. The command could be as simple as a cp, or it could invoke a complex shell script—it's all up to you.

The shell command to use is specified by the `archive_command` configuration parameter, which in practice will always be placed in the 'postgresql.conf' file. In this string, any %p is replaced by the path name of the file to archive, while any %f is replaced by the file name only. (The path name is relative to the working directory of the server, i.e., the cluster's data directory.) Write %% if you need to embed an actual % character in the command. The simplest useful command is something like

```
archive_command = 'cp -i %p /mnt/server/archivedir/%f </dev/null'
```

which will copy archivable WAL segments to the directory '/mnt/server/archivedir'. (This is an example, not a recommendation, and may not work on all platforms.)

The archive command will be executed under the ownership of the same user that the PostgreSQL server is running as. Since the series of WAL files being archived contains effectively everything in your database, you will want to be sure that the archived data is protected from prying eyes; for example, archive into a directory that does not have group or world read access.

It is important that the archive command return zero exit status if and only if it succeeded. Upon getting a zero result, PostgreSQL will assume that the WAL segment file has been successfully archived, and will remove or recycle it. However, a nonzero status tells PostgreSQL that the file was not archived; it will try again periodically until it succeeds.

The archive command should generally be designed to refuse to overwrite any pre-existing archive file. This is an important safety feature to preserve the integrity of your archive in case of administrator error (such as sending the output of two different servers to the same archive directory). It is advisable to test your proposed archive command to ensure that it indeed does not overwrite an existing file, *and that it returns nonzero status in this case.* We have found that cp -i does this correctly on some platforms but not others. If the chosen command does not itself handle this case correctly, you should add a command to test for pre-existence of the archive file. For example, something like

```
archive_command = 'test ! -f .../%f && cp %p .../%f'
```
works correctly on most Unix variants.

While designing your archiving setup, consider what will happen if the archive command fails repeatedly because some aspect requires operator intervention or the archive runs out of space. For example, this could occur if you write to tape without an autochanger; when the tape fills, nothing further can be archived until the tape is swapped. You should ensure that any error condition or request to a human operator is reported appropriately so that the situation can be resolved relatively quickly. The 'pg_xlog/' directory will continue to fill with WAL segment files until the situation is resolved.

The speed of the archiving command is not important, so long as it can keep up with the average rate at which your server generates WAL data. Normal operation continues even if the archiving process falls a little behind. If archiving falls significantly behind, this will increase the amount of data that would be lost in the event of a disaster. It will also mean that the 'pg_xlog/' directory will contain large numbers of not-yet-archived segment files, which could eventually exceed available disk space. You are advised to monitor the archiving process to ensure that it is working as you intend.

In writing your archive command, you should assume that the file names to be archived may be up to 64 characters long and may contain any combination of ASCII letters, digits, and dots. It is not necessary to remember the original relative path (%p) but it is necessary to remember the file name (%f).

Note that although WAL archiving will allow you to restore any modifications made to the data in your PostgreSQL database, it will not restore changes made to configuration files (that is, 'postgresql.conf', 'pg_hba.conf' and 'pg_ident.conf'), since those are edited manually rather than through SQL operations. You may wish to keep the configuration files in a location that will be backed up by your regular file system backup procedures. See Section 4.2 *File Locations*, page 47 for how to relocate the configuration files.

The archive command is only invoked on completed WAL segments. Hence, if your server generates only little WAL traffic (or has slack periods where it does so), there could be a long delay between the completion of a transaction and its safe recording in archive storage. To put a limit on how old unarchived data can be, you can set `archive_timeout` to force the server to switch to a new WAL segment file at least that often. Note that archived files that are ended early due to a forced switch are still the same length as completely full files. It is therefore unwise to set a very short `archive_timeout`—it will bloat your archive storage. `archive_timeout` settings of a minute or so are usually reasonable.

Also, you can force a segment switch manually with `pg_switch_xlog`, if you want to ensure that a just-finished transaction is archived immediately. Other utility functions related to WAL management are listed in Table 7.47.

10.3.2 Making a Base Backup

The procedure for making a base backup is relatively simple:

1. Ensure that WAL archiving is enabled and working.

2. Connect to the database as a superuser, and issue the command

    ```
    SELECT pg_start_backup('label');
    ```

    where `label` is any string you want to use to uniquely identify this backup operation. (One good practice is to use the full path where you intend to put the backup dump file.) `pg_start_backup` creates a *backup label* file, called 'backup_label', in the cluster directory with information about your backup.

    It does not matter which database within the cluster you connect to to issue this command. You can ignore the result returned by the function; but if it reports an error, deal with that before proceeding.

3. Perform the backup, using any convenient file-system-backup tool such as tar or cpio. It is neither necessary nor desirable to stop normal operation of the database while you do this.

4. Again connect to the database as a superuser, and issue the command

    ```
    SELECT pg_stop_backup();
    ```

    This terminates the backup mode and performs an automatic switch to the next WAL segment. The reason for the switch is to arrange that the last WAL segment file written during the backup interval is immediately ready to archive.

5. Once the WAL segment files used during the backup are archived, you are done. The file identified by `pg_stop_backup`'s result is the last segment that needs to be archived to complete the backup. Archival of these files will happen automatically, since you have already configured `archive_command`. In many cases, this happens fairly quickly, but you are advised to monitor your archival system to ensure this has taken place so that you can be certain you have a complete backup.

Some backup tools that you might wish to use emit warnings or errors if the files they are trying to copy change while the copy proceeds. This situation is normal, and not an error, when taking a base backup of an active database; so you need to ensure that you can distinguish complaints of this sort from real errors. For example, some versions of rsync return a separate exit code for "vanished source files", and you can write a driver script to accept this exit code as a non-error case. Also, some versions of GNU tar consider it an error if a file is changed while tar is copying it. There does not seem to be any very convenient way to distinguish this error from other types of errors, other than manual inspection of tar's messages. GNU tar is therefore not the best tool for making base backups.

It is not necessary to be very concerned about the amount of time elapsed between pg_start_backup and the start of the actual backup, nor between the end of the backup and pg_stop_backup; a few minutes' delay won't hurt anything. (However, if you normally run the server with full_page_writes disabled, you may notice a drop in performance between pg_start_backup and pg_stop_backup, since full_page_writes is effectively forced on during backup mode.) You must ensure that these steps are carried out in sequence without any possible overlap, or you will invalidate the backup.

Be certain that your backup dump includes all of the files underneath the database cluster directory (e.g., '/usr/local/pgsql/data'). If you are using tablespaces that do not reside underneath this directory, be careful to include them as well (and be sure that your backup dump archives symbolic links as links, otherwise the restore will mess up your tablespaces).

You may, however, omit from the backup dump the files within the 'pg_xlog/' subdirectory of the cluster directory. This slight complication is worthwhile because it reduces the risk of mistakes when restoring. This is easy to arrange if 'pg_xlog/' is a symbolic link pointing to someplace outside the cluster directory, which is a common setup anyway for performance reasons.

To make use of the backup, you will need to keep around all the WAL segment files generated during and after the file system backup. To aid you in doing this, the pg_stop_backup function creates a *backup history file* that is immediately stored into the WAL archive area. This file is named after the first WAL segment file that you need to have to make use of the backup. For example, if the starting WAL file is 0000000100001234000055CD the backup history file will be named something like 0000000100001234000055CD.007C9330.backup. (The second number in the file name stands for an exact position within the WAL file, and can ordinarily be ignored.) Once you have safely archived the file system backup and the WAL segment files used during the backup (as specified in the backup history file), all archived WAL segments with names numerically less are no longer needed to recover the file system backup and may be deleted. However, you should consider keeping several backup sets to be absolutely certain that you can recover your data.

The backup history file is just a small text file. It contains the label string you gave to pg_start_backup, as well as the starting and ending times and WAL segments of the backup. If you used the label to identify where the associated dump file is kept, then the archived history file is enough to tell you which dump file to restore, should you need to do so.

Since you have to keep around all the archived WAL files back to your last base backup, the interval between base backups should usually be chosen based on how much storage you want to expend on archived WAL files. You should also consider how long you are prepared to spend recovering, if recovery should be necessary—the system will have to replay all those WAL segments, and that could take awhile if it has been a long time since the last base backup.

It's also worth noting that the `pg_start_backup` function makes a file named 'backup_label' in the database cluster directory, which is then removed again by `pg_stop_backup`. This file will of course be archived as a part of your backup dump file. The backup label file includes the label string you gave to `pg_start_backup`, as well as the time at which `pg_start_backup` was run, and the name of the starting WAL file. In case of confusion it will therefore be possible to look inside a backup dump file and determine exactly which backup session the dump file came from.

It is also possible to make a backup dump while the server is stopped. In this case, you obviously cannot use `pg_start_backup` or `pg_stop_backup`, and you will therefore be left to your own devices to keep track of which backup dump is which and how far back the associated WAL files go. It is generally better to follow the continuous archiving procedure above.

10.3.3 Recovering using a Continuous Archive Backup

Okay, the worst has happened and you need to recover from your backup. Here is the procedure:

1. Stop the server, if it's running.

2. If you have the space to do so, copy the whole cluster data directory and any tablespaces to a temporary location in case you need them later. Note that this precaution will require that you have enough free space on your system to hold two copies of your existing database. If you do not have enough space, you need at the least to copy the contents of the 'pg_xlog' subdirectory of the cluster data directory, as it may contain logs which were not archived before the system went down.

3. Clean out all existing files and subdirectories under the cluster data directory and under the root directories of any tablespaces you are using.

4. Restore the database files from your backup dump. Be careful that they are restored with the right ownership (the database system user, not root!) and with the right permissions. If you are using tablespaces, you should verify that the symbolic links in 'pg_tblspc/' were correctly restored.

5. Remove any files present in 'pg_xlog/'; these came from the backup dump and are therefore probably obsolete rather than current. If you didn't archive 'pg_xlog/' at all, then recreate it, and be sure to recreate the subdirectory 'pg_xlog/archive_status/' as well.

6. If you had unarchived WAL segment files that you saved in step 2, copy them into 'pg_xlog/'. (It is best to copy them, not move them, so that you still have the unmodified files if a problem occurs and you have to start over.)

7. Create a recovery command file 'recovery.conf' in the cluster data directory (see Section 10.3.3.1 *Recovery Settings*, page 142). You may also want to temporarily modify 'pg_hba.conf' to prevent ordinary users from connecting until you are sure the recovery has worked.

8. Start the server. The server will go into recovery mode and proceed to read through the archived WAL files it needs. Should the recovery be terminated because of an external error, the server can simply be restarted and it will continue recovery. Upon completion of the recovery process, the server will rename 'recovery.conf' to 'recovery.done' (to prevent accidentally re-entering recovery mode in case of a crash later) and then commence normal database operations.

9. Inspect the contents of the database to ensure you have recovered to where you want to be. If not, return to step 1. If all is well, let in your users by restoring 'pg_hba.conf' to normal.

The key part of all this is to setup a recovery command file that describes how you want to recover and how far the recovery should run. You can use 'recovery.conf.sample' (normally installed in the installation 'share/' directory) as a prototype. The one thing that you absolutely must specify in 'recovery.conf' is the restore_command, which tells PostgreSQL how to get back archived WAL file segments. Like the archive_command, this is a shell command string. It may contain %f, which is replaced by the name of the desired log file, and %p, which is replaced by the path name to copy the log file to. (The path name is relative to the working directory of the server, i.e., the cluster's data directory.) Write %% if you need to embed an actual % character in the command. The simplest useful command is something like

```
restore_command = 'cp /mnt/server/archivedir/%f %p'
```

which will copy previously archived WAL segments from the directory '/mnt/server/archivedir'. You could of course use something much more complicated, perhaps even a shell script that requests the operator to mount an appropriate tape.

It is important that the command return nonzero exit status on failure. The command *will* be asked for log files that are not present in the archive; it must return nonzero when so asked. This is not an error condition. Be aware also that the base name of the %p path will be different from %f; do not expect them to be interchangeable.

WAL segments that cannot be found in the archive will be sought in 'pg_xlog/'; this allows use of recent un-archived segments. However segments that are available from the archive will be used in preference to files in 'pg_xlog/'. The system will not overwrite the existing contents of 'pg_xlog/' when retrieving archived files.

Normally, recovery will proceed through all available WAL segments, thereby restoring the database to the current point in time (or as close as we can get given the available WAL segments). But if you want to recover to some previous point in time (say, right before the junior DBA dropped your main transaction table), just specify the required stopping point in 'recovery.conf'. You can specify the stop point, known as the "recovery target", either by date/time or by completion of a specific transaction ID. As of this writing only the date/time option is very usable, since there are no tools to help you identify with any accuracy which transaction ID to use.

> Note: The stop point must be after the ending time of the base backup (the time of pg_stop_backup). You cannot use a base backup to recover to a time when that backup was still going on. (To recover to such a time, you must go back to your previous base backup and roll forward from there.)

If recovery finds a corruption in the WAL data then recovery will complete at that point and the server will not start. In such a case the recovery process could be re-run from the beginning, specifying a "recovery target" before the point of corruption so that recovery can complete normally. If recovery fails for an external reason, such as a system crash or if the WAL archive has become inaccessible, then the recovery can simply be restarted and it will restart almost from where it failed. Recovery restart works much like checkpointing in normal operation: the server periodically forces all its state to disk, and then updates the 'pg_control' file to indicate that the already-processed WAL data need not be scanned again.

10.3.3.1 Recovery Settings

These settings can only be made in the 'recovery.conf' file, and apply only for the duration of the recovery. They must be reset for any subsequent recovery you wish to perform. They cannot be changed once recovery has begun.

restore_command (string)

> The shell command to execute to retrieve an archived segment of the WAL file series. This parameter is required. Any %f in the string is replaced by the name of the file to retrieve from the archive, and any %p is replaced by the path name to copy it to on the server. (The path name is relative to the working directory of the server, i.e., the cluster's data directory.) Write %% to embed an actual % character in the command.
>
> It is important for the command to return a zero exit status if and only if it succeeds. The command *will* be asked for file names that are not present in the archive; it must return nonzero when so asked. Examples:
>
> ```
> restore_command = 'cp /mnt/server/archivedir/%f "%p"'
> restore_command = 'copy /mnt/server/archivedir/%f "%p"'
> # Windows
> ```

recovery_target_time (timestamp)

> This parameter specifies the time stamp up to which recovery will proceed. At most one of recovery_target_time and recovery_target_xid can be specified. The default is to recover to the end of the WAL log. The precise stopping point is also influenced by recovery_target_inclusive.

recovery_target_xid (string)

This parameter specifies the transaction ID up to which recovery will proceed. Keep in mind that while transaction IDs are assigned sequentially at transaction start, transactions can complete in a different numeric order. The transactions that will be recovered are those that committed before (and optionally including) the specified one. At most one of recovery_target_xid and recovery_target_time can be specified. The default is to recover to the end of the WAL log. The precise stopping point is also influenced by recovery_target_inclusive.

recovery_target_inclusive (boolean)

Specifies whether we stop just after the specified recovery target (true), or just before the recovery target (false). Applies to both recovery_target_time and recovery_target_xid, whichever one is specified for this recovery. This indicates whether transactions having exactly the target commit time or ID, respectively, will be included in the recovery. Default is true.

recovery_target_timeline (string)

Specifies recovering into a particular timeline. The default is to recover along the same timeline that was current when the base backup was taken. You would only need to set this parameter in complex re-recovery situations, where you need to return to a state that itself was reached after a point-in-time recovery. See Section 10.3.4 *Timelines* for discussion.

10.3.4 Timelines

The ability to restore the database to a previous point in time creates some complexities that are akin to science-fiction stories about time travel and parallel universes. In the original history of the database, perhaps you dropped a critical table at 5:15PM on Tuesday evening. Unfazed, you get out your backup, restore to the point-in-time 5:14PM Tuesday evening, and are up and running. In *this* history of the database universe, you never dropped the table at all. But suppose you later realize this wasn't such a great idea after all, and would like to return to some later point in the original history. You won't be able to if, while your database was up-and-running, it overwrote some of the sequence of WAL segment files that led up to the time you now wish you could get back to. So you really want to distinguish the series of WAL records generated after you've done a point-in-time recovery from those that were generated in the original database history.

To deal with these problems, PostgreSQL has a notion of *timelines*. Each time you recover to a point-in-time earlier than the end of the WAL sequence, a new timeline is created to identify the series of WAL records generated after that recovery. (If recovery proceeds all the way to the end of WAL, however, we do not start a new timeline: we just extend the existing one.) The timeline ID number is part of WAL segment file names, and so a new timeline does not overwrite the WAL data generated by previous timelines. It is in fact possible to archive many different timelines. While that might seem like a useless feature, it's often a lifesaver. Consider the situation where you aren't quite sure what point-in-time to recover to, and so have to do several point-in-time recoveries by trial and error until you find the best place to branch off from the old history. Without timelines this process would soon generate an unmanageable mess. With timelines, you can recover to *any* prior state, including states in timeline branches that you later abandoned.

Each time a new timeline is created, PostgreSQL creates a "timeline history" file that shows which timeline it branched off from and when. These history files are necessary to allow the system to pick the right WAL segment files when recovering from an archive that contains multiple timelines. Therefore, they are archived into the WAL archive area just like WAL segment files. The history files are just small text files, so it's cheap and appropriate to keep them around indefinitely (unlike the segment files which are large). You can, if you like, add comments to a history file to make your own notes about how and why this particular timeline came to be. Such comments will be especially valuable when you have a thicket of different timelines as a result of experimentation.

The default behavior of recovery is to recover along the same timeline that was current when the base backup was taken. If you want to recover into some child timeline (that is, you want to return to some state that was itself generated after a recovery attempt), you need to specify the target timeline ID in 'recovery.conf'. You cannot recover into timelines that branched off earlier than the base backup.

10.3.5 Caveats

At this writing, there are several limitations of the continuous archiving technique. These will probably be fixed in future releases:

- Operations on hash indexes are not presently WAL-logged, so replay will not update these indexes. The recommended workaround is to manually REINDEX each such index after completing a recovery operation.

- If a CREATE DATABASE command is executed while a base backup is being taken, and then the template database that the CREATE DATABASE copied is modified while the base backup is still in progress, it is possible that recovery will cause those modifications to be propagated into the created database as well. This is of course undesirable. To avoid this risk, it is best not to modify any template databases while taking a base backup.

- CREATE TABLESPACE commands are WAL-logged with the literal absolute path, and will therefore be replayed as tablespace creations with the same absolute path. This might be undesirable if the log is being replayed on a different machine. It can be dangerous even if the log is being replayed on the same machine, but into a new data directory: the replay will still over-write the contents of the original tablespace. To avoid potential gotchas of this sort, the best practice is to take a new base backup after creating or dropping tablespaces.

It should also be noted that the default WAL format is fairly bulky since it includes many disk page snapshots. These page snapshots are designed to support crash recovery, since we may need to fix partially-written disk pages. Depending on your system hardware and software, the risk of partial writes may be small enough to ignore, in which case you can significantly reduce the total volume of archived logs by turning off page snapshots using the full_page_ writes parameter. (Read the notes and warnings in Chapter 14 *Reliability and the Write-Ahead Log*, page 171 before you do so.) Turning off page snapshots does not prevent use of the logs for PITR operations. An area for future development is to compress archived WAL data by removing unnecessary page copies even when full_page_writes is on. In the meantime, administrators may wish to reduce the number of page snapshots included in WAL by increasing the checkpoint interval parameters as much as feasible.

10.4 Warm Standby Servers for High Availability

Continuous archiving can be used to create a *high availability* (HA) cluster configuration with one or more *standby servers* ready to take over operations if the primary server fails. This capability is widely referred to as *warm standby* or *log shipping*.

The primary and standby server work together to provide this capability, though the servers are only loosely coupled. The primary server operates in continuous archiving mode, while each standby server operates in continuous recovery mode, reading the WAL files from the primary. No changes to the database tables are required to enable this capability, so it offers low administration overhead in comparison with some other replication approaches. This configuration also has relatively low performance impact on the primary server.

Directly moving WAL or "log" records from one database server to another is typically described as log shipping. PostgreSQL implements file-based log shipping, which means that WAL records are transferred one file (WAL segment) at a time. WAL files can be shipped easily and cheaply over any distance, whether it be to an adjacent system, another system on the same site or another system on the far side of the globe. The bandwidth required for this technique varies according to the transaction rate of the primary server. Record-based log shipping is also possible with custom-developed procedures, as discussed in Section 10.4.4 *Record-based Log Shipping*, page 148.

It should be noted that the log shipping is asynchronous, i.e. the WAL records are shipped after transaction commit. As a result there is a window for data loss should the primary server suffer a catastrophic failure: transactions not yet shipped will be lost. The length of the window of data loss can be limited by use of the archive_timeout parameter, which can be set as low as a few seconds if required. However such low settings will substantially increase the bandwidth requirements for file shipping. If you need a window of less than a minute or so, it's probably better to look into record-based log shipping.

The standby server is not available for access, since it is continually performing recovery processing. Recovery performance is sufficiently good that the standby will typically be only moments away from full availability once it has been activated. As a result, we refer to this capability as a warm standby configuration that offers high availability. Restoring a server from an archived base backup and rollforward will take considerably longer, so that technique only really offers a solution for disaster recovery, not HA.

10.4.1 Planning

It is usually wise to create the primary and standby servers so that they are as similar as possible, at least from the perspective of the database server. In particular, the path names associated with tablespaces will be passed across as-is, so both primary and standby servers must have the same mount paths for tablespaces if that feature is used. Keep in mind that if CREATE TABLESPACE is executed on the primary, any new mount point needed for it must be created on both the primary and all standby servers before the command is executed. Hardware need not be exactly the same, but experience shows that maintaining two identical systems is easier than maintaining two dissimilar ones over the lifetime of the application and system. In any case the hardware architecture must be the same—shipping from, say, a 32-bit to a 64-bit system will not work.

In general, log shipping between servers running different major release levels will not be possible. It is the policy of the PostgreSQL Global Development Group not to make changes to disk formats during minor release upgrades, so it is likely that running different minor release levels on primary and standby servers will work successfully. However, no formal support for that is offered and you are advised to keep primary and standby servers at the same release level as much as possible. When updating to a new minor release, the safest policy is to update the standby servers first—a new minor release is more likely to be able to read WAL files from a previous minor release than vice versa.

There is no special mode required to enable a standby server. The operations that occur on both primary and standby servers are entirely normal continuous archiving and recovery tasks. The only point of contact between the two database servers is the archive of WAL files that both share: primary writing to the archive, standby reading from the archive. Care must be taken to ensure that WAL archives for separate primary servers do not become mixed together or confused.

The magic that makes the two loosely coupled servers work together is simply a restore_command used on the standby that waits for the next WAL file to become available from the primary. The restore_command is specified in the 'recovery.conf' file on the standby server. Normal recovery processing would request a file from the WAL archive, reporting failure if the file was unavailable. For standby processing it is normal for the next file to be unavailable, so we must be patient and wait for it to appear. A waiting restore_command can be written as a custom script that loops after polling for the existence of the next WAL file. There must also be some way to trigger failover, which should interrupt the restore_command, break the loop and return a file-not-found error to the standby server. This ends recovery and the standby will then come up as a normal server.

Pseudocode for a suitable restore_command is:

```
triggered = false;
while (!NextWALFileReady() && !triggered)
{
    sleep(100000L);          /* wait for ~0.1 sec */
    if (CheckForExternalTrigger())
        triggered = true;
```

```
      }
      if (!triggered)
            CopyWALFileForRecovery();
```

PostgreSQL does not provide the system software required to identify a failure on the primary and notify the standby system and then the standby database server. Many such tools exist and are well integrated with other aspects required for successful failover, such as IP address migration.

The means for triggering failover is an important part of planning and design. The `restore_command` is executed in full once for each WAL file. The process running the `restore_command` is therefore created and dies for each file, so there is no daemon or server process and so we cannot use signals and a signal handler. A more permanent notification is required to trigger the failover. It is possible to use a simple timeout facility, especially if used in conjunction with a known `archive_timeout` setting on the primary. This is somewhat error prone since a network problem or busy primary server might be sufficient to initiate failover. A notification mechanism such as the explicit creation of a trigger file is less error prone, if this can be arranged.

10.4.2 Implementation

The short procedure for configuring a standby server is as follows. For full details of each step, refer to previous sections as noted.

1. Set up primary and standby systems as near identically as possible, including two identical copies of PostgreSQL at the same release level.

2. Set up continuous archiving from the primary to a WAL archive located in a directory on the standby server. Ensure that `archive_command` and `archive_timeout` are set appropriately on the primary (see Section 10.3.1 *Setting up WAL archiving*, page 136).

3. Make a base backup of the primary server (see Section 10.3.2 *Making a Base Backup*, page 138), and load this data onto the standby.

4. Begin recovery on the standby server from the local WAL archive, using a 'recovery.conf' that specifies a `restore_command` that waits as described previously (see Section 10.3.3 *Recovering using a Continuous Archive Backup*, page 140).

Recovery treats the WAL archive as read-only, so once a WAL file has been copied to the standby system it can be copied to tape at the same time as it is being read by the standby database server. Thus, running a standby server for high availability can be performed at the same time as files are stored for longer term disaster recovery purposes.

For testing purposes, it is possible to run both primary and standby servers on the same system. This does not provide any worthwhile improvement in server robustness, nor would it be described as HA.

10.4.3 Failover

If the primary server fails then the standby server should begin failover procedures.

If the standby server fails then no failover need take place. If the standby server can be restarted, even some time later, then the recovery process can also be immediately restarted, taking advantage of restartable recovery. If the standby server cannot be restarted, then a full new standby server should be created.

If the primary server fails and then immediately restarts, you must have a mechanism for informing it that it is no longer the primary. This is sometimes known as STONITH (Shoot the Other Node In The Head), which is necessary to avoid situations where both systems think they are the primary, which can lead to confusion and ultimately data loss.

Many failover systems use just two systems, the primary and the standby, connected by some kind of heartbeat mechanism to continually verify the connectivity between the two and the viability of the primary. It is also possible to use a third system (called a witness server) to avoid some problems of inappropriate failover, but the additional complexity may not be worthwhile unless it is set-up with sufficient care and rigorous testing.

Once failover to the standby occurs, we have only a single server in operation. This is known as a degenerate state. The former standby is now the primary, but the former primary is down and may stay down. To return to normal operation we must fully recreate a standby server, either on the former primary system when it comes up, or on a third, possibly new, system. Once complete the primary and standby can be considered to have switched roles. Some people choose to use a third server to provide backup to the new primary until the new standby server is recreated, though clearly this complicates the system configuration and operational processes.

So, switching from primary to standby server can be fast but requires some time to re-prepare the failover cluster. Regular switching from primary to standby is encouraged, since it allows regular downtime on each system for maintenance. This also acts as a test of the failover mechanism to ensure that it will really work when you need it. Written administration procedures are advised.

10.4.4 Record-based Log Shipping

PostgreSQL directly supports file-based log shipping as described above. It is also possible to implement record-based log shipping, though this requires custom development.

An external program can call the `pg_xlogfile_name_offset()` function (see Volume 1, Section 7.20 *System Administration Functions*) to find out the file name and the exact byte offset within it of the current end of WAL. It can then access the WAL file directly and copy the data from the last known end of WAL through the current end over to the standby server(s). With this approach, the window for data loss is the polling cycle time of the copying program, which can be very small, but there is no wasted bandwidth from forcing partially-used segment files to be archived. Note that the standby servers' `restore_command` scripts still deal in whole WAL files, so the incrementally copied data is not ordinarily made available to the standby servers. It is of use only when the primary dies—then the last partial WAL file is fed to the standby before allowing it to come up. So correct implementation of this process requires cooperation of the `restore_command` script with the data copying program.

10.4.5 Incrementally Updated Backups

In a warm standby configuration, it is possible to offload the expense of taking periodic base backups from the primary server; instead base backups can be made by backing up a standby server's files. This concept is generally known as incrementally updated backups, log change accumulation or more simply, change accumulation.

If we take a backup of the standby server's files while it is following logs shipped from the primary, we will be able to reload that data and restart the standby's recovery process from the last restart point. We no longer need to keep WAL files from before the restart point. If we need to recover, it will be faster to recover from the incrementally updated backup than from the original base backup.

Since the standby server is not "live", it is not possible to use `pg_start_backup()` and `pg_stop_backup()` to manage the backup process; it will be up to you to determine how far back you need to keep WAL segment files to have a recoverable backup. You can do this by running pg_controldata on the standby server to inspect the control file and determine the current checkpoint WAL location.

10.5 Migration Between Releases

This section discusses how to migrate your database data from one Post-greSQL release to a newer one. The software installation procedure *per se* is not the subject of this section; those details are in Chapter 1 *Installation Instructions*, page 5.

As a general rule, the internal data storage format is subject to change between major releases of PostgreSQL (where the number after the first dot changes). This does not apply to different minor releases under the same major release (where the number after the second dot changes); these always have compatible storage formats. For example, releases 7.2.1, 7.3.2, and 7.4 are not compatible, whereas 7.2.1 and 7.2.2 are. When you update between compatible versions, you can simply replace the executables and reuse the data directory on disk. Otherwise you need to back up your data and restore it on the new server. This has to be done using pg_dump; file system level backup methods obviously won't work. There are checks in place that prevent you from using a data directory with an incompatible version of PostgreSQL, so no great harm can be done by trying to start the wrong server version on a data directory.

It is recommended that you use the pg_dump and pg_dumpall programs from the newer version of PostgreSQL, to take advantage of any enhancements that may have been made in these programs. Current releases of the dump programs can read data from any server version back to 7.0.

The least downtime can be achieved by installing the new server in a different directory and running both the old and the new servers in parallel, on different ports. Then you can use something like

```
pg_dumpall -p 5432 | psql -d postgres -p 6543
```

to transfer your data. Or use an intermediate file if you want. Then you can shut down the old server and start the new server at the port the old one was running at. You should make sure that the old database is not updated after you run pg_dumpall, otherwise you will obviously lose that data. See Chapter 7 *Client Authentication*, page 99 for information on how to prohibit access.

In practice you probably want to test your client applications on the new setup before switching over completely. This is another reason for setting up concurrent installations of old and new versions.

If you cannot or do not want to run two servers in parallel you can do the backup step before installing the new version, bring down the server, move the old version out of the way, install the new version, start the new server, restore the data. For example:

```
pg_dumpall > backup
pg_ctl stop
mv /usr/local/pgsql /usr/local/pgsql.old
cd ~/postgresql-8.2.4
gmake install
initdb -D /usr/local/pgsql/data
postgres -D /usr/local/pgsql/data
psql -f backup postgres
```

See Chapter 3 *Operating System Environment*, page 27 about ways to start and stop the server and other details. The installation instructions will advise you of strategic places to perform these steps.

> **Note:** When you "move the old installation out of the way" it may no longer be perfectly usable. Some of the executable programs contain absolute paths to various installed programs and data files. This is usually not a big problem but if you plan on using two installations in parallel for a while you should assign them different installation directories at build time. (This problem is rectified in PostgreSQL 8.0 and later, but you need to be wary of moving older installations.)

11 High Availability and Load Balancing

Database servers can work together to allow a second server to take over quickly if the primary server fails (high availability), or to allow several computers to serve the same data (load balancing). Ideally, database servers could work together seamlessly. Web servers serving static web pages can be combined quite easily by merely load-balancing web requests to multiple machines. In fact, read-only database servers can be combined relatively easily too. Unfortunately, most database servers have a read/write mix of requests, and read/write servers are much harder to combine. This is because though read-only data needs to be placed on each server only once, a write to any server has to be propagated to all servers so that future read requests to those servers return consistent results.

This synchronization problem is the fundamental difficulty for servers working together. Because there is no single solution that eliminates the impact of the sync problem for all use cases, there are multiple solutions. Each solution addresses this problem in a different way, and minimizes its impact for a specific workload.

Some solutions deal with synchronization by allowing only one server to modify the data. Servers that can modify data are called read/write or "master" servers. Servers that can reply to read-only queries are called "slave" servers. Servers that cannot be accessed until they are changed to master servers are called "standby" servers.

Some failover and load balancing solutions are synchronous, meaning that a data-modifying transaction is not considered committed until all servers have committed the transaction. This guarantees that a failover will not lose any data and that all load-balanced servers will return consistent results no matter which server is queried. In contrast, asynchronous solutions allow some delay between the time of a commit and its propagation to the other servers, opening the possibility that some transactions might be lost in the switch to a backup server, and that load balanced servers might return slightly stale results. Asynchronous communication is used when synchronous would be too slow.

Solutions can also be categorized by their granularity. Some solutions can deal only with an entire database server, while others allow control at the per-table or per-database level.

Performance must be considered in any failover or load balancing choice. There is usually a tradeoff between functionality and performance. For example, a full synchronous solution over a slow network might cut performance by more than half, while an asynchronous one might have a minimal performance impact.

The remainder of this section outlines various failover, replication, and load balancing solutions.

Shared Disk Failover

Shared disk failover avoids synchronization overhead by having only one copy of the database. It uses a single disk array that is shared by multiple servers. If the main database server fails, the standby server is able to mount and start the database as though it was recovering from a database crash. This allows rapid failover with no data loss.

Shared hardware functionality is common in network storage devices. Using a network file system is also possible, though care must be taken that the file system has full POSIX behavior. One significant limitation of this method is that if the shared disk array fails or becomes corrupt, the primary and standby servers are both nonfunctional. Another issue is that the standby server should never access the shared storage while the primary server is running.

A modified version of shared hardware functionality is file system replication, where all changes to a file system are mirrored to a file system residing on another computer. The only restriction is that the mirroring must be done in a way that ensures the standby server has a consistent copy of the file system—specifically, writes to the standby must be done in the same order as those on the master. DRBD is a popular file system replication solution for Linux.

Warm Standby Using Point-In-Time Recovery

A warm standby server (see Section 10.4 *Warm Standby Servers for High Availability*, page 145) can be kept current by reading a stream of write-ahead log (WAL) records. If the main server fails, the warm standby contains almost all of the data of the main server, and can be quickly made the new master database server. This is asynchronous and can only be done for the entire database server.

Master-Slave Replication

A master-slave replication setup sends all data modification queries to the master server. The master server asynchronously sends data changes to the slave server. The slave can answer read-only queries while the master server is running. The slave server is ideal for data warehouse queries.

Slony-I is an example of this type of replication, with per-table granularity, and support for multiple slaves. Because it updates the slave server asynchronously (in batches), there is possible data loss during fail over.

Statement-Based Replication Middleware

With statement-based replication middleware, a program intercepts every SQL query and sends it to one or all servers. Each server operates independently. Read-write queries are sent to all servers, while read-only queries can be sent to just one server, allowing the read workload to be distributed.

If queries are simply broadcast unmodified, functions like random(), CURRENT_TIMESTAMP, and sequences would have different values on different servers. This is because each server operates independently, and because SQL queries are broadcast (and not actual modified rows). If this is unacceptable, either the middleware or the application must query such values from a single server and then use those values in write queries. Also, care must be taken that all transactions either commit or abort on all servers, perhaps using two-phase commit (PREPARE TRANSACTION and COMMIT PREPARED. Pgpool and Sequoia are an example of this type of replication.

Synchronous Multi-Master Replication

In synchronous multi-master replication, each server can accept write requests, and modified data is transmitted from the original server to every other server before each transaction commits. Heavy write activity can cause excessive locking, leading to poor performance. In fact, write performance is often worse than that of a single server. Read requests can be sent to any server. Some implementations use shared disk to reduce the communication overhead. Synchronous multi-master replication is best for mostly read workloads, though its big advantage is that any server can accept write requests—there is no need to partition workloads between master and slave servers, and because the data changes are sent from one server to another, there is no problem with non-deterministic functions like random().

PostgreSQL does not offer this type of replication, though PostgreSQL two-phase commit (PREPARE TRANSACTION and COMMIT PREPARED) can be used to implement this in application code or middleware.

Asynchronous Multi-Master Replication

For servers that are not regularly connected, like laptops or remote servers, keeping data consistent among servers is a challenge. Using asynchronous multi-master replication, each server works independently, and periodically communicates with the other servers to identify conflicting transactions. The conflicts can be resolved by users or conflict resolution rules.

Data Partitioning

Data partitioning splits tables into data sets. Each set can be modified by only one server. For example, data can be partitioned by offices, e.g. London and Paris, with a server in each office. If queries combining London and Paris data are necessary, an application can query both servers, or master/slave replication can be used to keep a read-only copy of the other office's data on each server.

Multi-Server Parallel Query Execution

Many of the above solutions allow multiple servers to handle multiple queries, but none allow a single query to use multiple servers to complete faster. This solution allows multiple servers to work concurrently on a single query. This is usually accomplished by splitting the data among servers and having each server execute its part of the query and return results to a central server where they are combined and returned to the user. Pgpool-II has this capability.

Commercial Solutions

Because PostgreSQL is open source and easily extended, a number of companies have taken PostgreSQL and created commercial closed-source solutions with unique failover, replication, and load balancing capabilities.

12 Monitoring Database Activity

A database administrator frequently wonders, "What is the system doing right now?" This chapter discusses how to find that out.

Several tools are available for monitoring database activity and analyzing performance. Most of this chapter is devoted to describing PostgreSQL's statistics collector, but one should not neglect regular Unix monitoring programs such as ps, top, iostat, and vmstat. Also, once one has identified a poorly-performing query, further investigation may be needed using PostgreSQL's EXPLAIN command. Volume 1, Section 11.1 *Using EXPLAIN* discusses EXPLAIN and other methods for understanding the behavior of an individual query.

12.1 Standard Unix Tools

On most platforms, PostgreSQL modifies its command title as reported by ps, so that individual server processes can readily be identified. A sample display is

```
$ ps auxww | grep ^postgres
postgres   960  0.0  1.1  6104 1480 pts/1     SN    13:17
 0:00 postgres -i
postgres   963  0.0  1.1  7084 1472 pts/1     SN    13:17
 0:00 postgres: writer process
postgres   965  0.0  1.1  6152 1512 pts/1     SN    13:17
 0:00 postgres: stats collector process
postgres   998  0.0  2.3  6532 2992 pts/1     SN    13:18
 0:00 postgres: tgl runbug 127.0.0.1 idle
postgres  1003  0.0  2.4  6532 3128 pts/1     SN    13:19
 0:00 postgres: tgl regression [local] SELECT waiting
postgres  1016  0.1  2.4  6532 3080 pts/1     SN    13:19
 0:00 postgres: tgl regression [local] idle in transaction
```

(The appropriate invocation of ps varies across different platforms, as do the details of what is shown. This example is from a recent Linux system.) The first process listed here is the master server process. The command arguments shown for it are the same ones given when it was launched. The next two processes are background worker processes automatically launched by the master process. (The "stats collector" process will not be present if you have set the system not to start the statistics collector.) Each of the remaining processes is a server process handling one client connection. Each such process sets its command line display in the form

```
postgres: user database host activity
```

The user, database, and connection source host items remain the same for the life of the client connection, but the activity indicator changes. The activity may be idle (i.e., waiting for a client command), idle in transaction (waiting for client inside a BEGIN block), or a command type name such as SELECT. Also, waiting is attached if the server process is presently waiting on a lock held by another server process. In the above example we can infer that process 1003 is waiting for process 1016 to complete its transaction and thereby release some lock or other.

If you have turned off `update_process_title` then the activity indicator is not updated; the process title is set only once when a new process is launched. On some platforms this saves a useful amount of per-command overhead, on others it's insignificant.

> **Tip:** Solaris requires special handling. You must use /usr/ucb/ps, rather than /bin/ps. You also must use two w flags, not just one. In addition, your original invocation of the `postgres` command must have a shorter ps status display than that provided by each server process. If you fail to do all three things, the ps output for each server process will be the original `postgres` command line.

12.2 The Statistics Collector

PostgreSQL's *statistics collector* is a subsystem that supports collection and reporting of information about server activity. Presently, the collector can count accesses to tables and indexes in both disk-block and individual-row terms.

PostgreSQL also supports determining the exact command currently being executed by other server processes. This is an independent facility that can be enabled or disabled whether or not block-level and row-level statistics are being collected.

12.2.1 Statistics Collection Configuration

Since collection of statistics adds some overhead to query execution, the system can be configured to collect or not collect information. This is controlled by configuration parameters that are normally set in 'postgresql.conf'. (See Chapter 4 *Server Configuration*, page 45 for details about setting configuration parameters.)

The parameter `stats_start_collector` must be set to true for the statistics collector to be launched at all. This is the default and recommended setting, but it may be turned off if you have no interest in statistics and want to squeeze out every last drop of overhead. (The savings is likely to be small, however.) Note that this option cannot be changed while the server is running.

The parameters `stats_block_level` and `stats_row_level` control how much information is actually sent to the collector and thus determine how much runtime overhead occurs. These respectively determine whether a server process tracks disk-block-level access statistics and row-level access statistics and sends these to the collector. Additionally, per-database transaction commit and abort statistics are collected if either of these parameters are set.

The parameter `stats_command_string` enables monitoring of the current command being executed by any server process. The statistics collector subprocess need not be running to enable this feature.

Normally these parameters are set in 'postgresql.conf' so that they apply to all server processes, but it is possible to turn them on or off in individual sessions using the SET command. (To prevent ordinary users from hiding their activity from the administrator, only superusers are allowed to change these parameters with SET.)

> **Note:** Since the parameters `stats_block_level`, and `stats_row_level` default to `false`, very few statistics are collected in the default configuration. Enabling either of these configuration variables will significantly increase the amount of useful data produced by the statistics facilities, at the expense of additional run-time overhead.

12.2.2 Viewing Collected Statistics

Several predefined views, listed in Table 12.1, are available to show the results of statistics collection. Alternatively, one can build custom views using the underlying statistics functions.

When using the statistics to monitor current activity, it is important to realize that the information does not update instantaneously. Each individual server process transmits new block and row access counts to the collector just before going idle; so a query or transaction still in progress does not affect the displayed totals. Also, the collector itself emits a new report at most once per `PGSTAT_STAT_INTERVAL` milliseconds (500 unless altered while building the server). So the displayed information lags behind actual activity. However, current-query information collected by `stats_command_string` is always up-to-date.

Another important point is that when a server process is asked to display any of these statistics, it first fetches the most recent report emitted by the collector process and then continues to use this snapshot for all statistical views and functions until the end of its current transaction. So the statistics will appear not to change as long as you continue the current transaction. Similarly, information about the current queries of all processes is collected when any such information is first requested within a transaction, and the same information will be displayed throughout the transaction. This is a feature, not a bug, because it allows you to perform several queries on the statistics and correlate the results without worrying that the numbers are changing underneath you. But if you want to see new results with each query, be sure to do the queries outside any transaction block.

VIEW NAME	DESCRIPTION
pg_stat_activity	One row per server process, showing database OID, database name, process ID, user OID, user name, current query, query's waiting status, time at which the current query began execution, time at which the process was started, and client's address and port number. The columns that report data on the current query are available unless the parameter stats_command_string has been turned off. Furthermore, these columns are only visible if the user examining the view is a superuser or the same as the user owning the process being reported on.
pg_stat_database	One row per database, showing database OID, database name, number of active server processes connected to that database, number of transactions committed and rolled back in that database, total disk blocks read, and total buffer hits (i.e., block read requests avoided by finding the block already in buffer cache).
pg_stat_all_tables	For each table in the current database (including TOAST tables), the table OID, schema and table name, number of sequential scans initiated, number of live rows fetched by sequential scans, number of index scans initiated (over all indexes belonging to the table), number of live rows fetched by index scans, numbers of row insertions, updates, and deletions, the last time the table was vacuumed manually, the last time it was vacuumed by the autovacuum daemon, the last time it was analyzed manually, and the last time it was analyzed by the autovacuum daemon.
pg_stat_sys_tables	Same as pg_stat_all_tables, except that only system tables are shown.
pg_stat_user_tables	Same as pg_stat_all_tables, except that only user tables are shown.
pg_stat_all_indexes	For each index in the current database, the table and index OID, schema, table and index name, number of index scans initiated on that index, number of index entries returned by index scans, and number of live table rows fetched by simple index scans using that index.

pg_stat_sys_indexes	Same as pg_stat_all_indexes, except that only indexes on system tables are shown.
pg_stat_user_indexes	Same as pg_stat_all_indexes, except that only indexes on user tables are shown.
pg_statio_all_tables	For each table in the current database (including TOAST tables), the table OID, schema and table name, number of disk blocks read from that table, number of buffer hits, numbers of disk blocks read and buffer hits in all indexes of that table, numbers of disk blocks read and buffer hits from that table's auxiliary TOAST table (if any), and numbers of disk blocks read and buffer hits for the TOAST table's index.
pg_statio_sys_tables	Same as pg_statio_all_tables, except that only system tables are shown.
pg_statio_user_tables	Same as pg_statio_all_tables, except that only user tables are shown.
pg_statio_all_indexes	For each index in the current database, the table and index OID, schema, table and index name, numbers of disk blocks read and buffer hits in that index.
pg_statio_sys_indexes	Same as pg_statio_all_indexes, except that only indexes on system tables are shown.
pg_statio_user_indexes	Same as pg_statio_all_indexes, except that only indexes on user tables are shown.
pg_statio_all_sequences	For each sequence object in the current database, the sequence OID, schema and sequence name, numbers of disk blocks read and buffer hits in that sequence.
pg_statio_sys_sequences	Same as pg_statio_all_sequences, except that only system sequences are shown. (Presently, no system sequences are defined, so this view is always empty.)
pg_statio_user_sequences	Same as pg_statio_all_sequences, except that only user sequences are shown.

Table 12.1: Standard Statistics Views

The per-index statistics are particularly useful to determine which indexes are being used and how effective they are.

Beginning in PostgreSQL 8.1, indexes can be used either directly or via "bitmap scans". In a bitmap scan the output of several indexes can be combined via AND or OR rules; so it is difficult to associate individual heap row fetches with specific indexes when a bitmap scan is used. Therefore, a bitmap scan increments the pg_stat_all_indexes.idx_tup_read count(s) for the index(es) it uses, and it increments the pg_stat_all_tables.idx_tup_fetch count for the table, but it does not affect pg_stat_all_indexes.idx_tup_fetch.

Note: Before PostgreSQL 8.1, the idx_tup_read and idx_tup_fetch counts were essentially always equal. Now they can be different even without considering bitmap scans, because idx_tup_read counts index entries retrieved from the index while idx_tup_fetch counts live rows fetched from the table; the latter will be less if any dead or not-yet-committed rows are fetched using the index.

The pg_statio_ views are primarily useful to determine the effectiveness of the buffer cache. When the number of actual disk reads is much smaller than the number of buffer hits, then the cache is satisfying most read requests without invoking a kernel call. However, these statistics do not give the entire story: due to the way in which PostgreSQL handles disk I/O, data that is not in the PostgreSQL buffer cache may still reside in the kernel's I/O cache, and may therefore still be fetched without requiring a physical read. Users interested in obtaining more detailed information on PostgreSQL I/O behavior are advised to use the PostgreSQL statistics collector in combination with operating system utilities that allow insight into the kernel's handling of I/O.

Other ways of looking at the statistics can be set up by writing queries that use the same underlying statistics access functions as these standard views do. These functions are listed in Table 12.2. The per-database access functions take a database OID as argument to identify which database to report on. The per-table and per-index functions take a table or index OID. (Note that only tables and indexes in the current database can be seen with these functions.) The per-server-process access functions take a server process number, which ranges from one to the number of currently active server processes.

FUNCTION	RETURN TYPE	DESCRIPTION
`pg_stat_get_db_numbackends(oid)`	integer	Number of active server processes for database
`pg_stat_get_db_xact_commit(oid)`	bigint	Transactions committed in database
`pg_stat_get_db_xact_rollback(oid)`	bigint	Transactions rolled back in database
`pg_stat_get_db_blocks_fetched(oid)`	bigint	Number of disk block fetch requests for database
`pg_stat_get_db_blocks_hit(oid)`	bigint	Number of disk block fetch requests found in cache for database
`pg_stat_get_numscans(oid)`	bigint	Number of sequential scans done when argument is a table, or number of index scans done when argument is an index
`pg_stat_get_tuples_returned(oid)`	bigint	Number of rows read by sequential scans when argument is a table, or number of index entries returned when argument is an index
`pg_stat_get_tuples_fetched(oid)`	bigint	Number of table rows fetched by bitmap scans when argument is a table, or table rows fetched by simple index scans using the index when argument is an index
`pg_stat_get_tuples_inserted(oid)`	bigint	Number of rows inserted into table
`pg_stat_get_tuples_updated(oid)`	bigint	Number of rows updated in table
`pg_stat_get_tuples_deleted(oid)`	bigint	Number of rows deleted from table
`pg_stat_get_blocks_fetched(oid)`	bigint	Number of disk block fetch requests for table or index

`pg_stat_get_blocks_hit(oid)`	`bigint`	Number of disk block requests found in cache for table or index
`pg_stat_get_last_vacuum_time(oid)`	`timestamptz`	Time of the last vacuum initiated by the user on this table
`pg_stat_get_last_autovacuum_time(oid)`	`timestamptz`	Time of the last vacuum initiated by the autovacuum daemon on this table
`pg_stat_get_last_analyze_time(oid)`	`timestamptz`	Time of the last analyze initiated by the user on this table
`pg_stat_get_last_autoanalyze_time(oid)`	`timestamptz`	Time of the last analyze initiated by the autovacuum daemon on this table
`pg_stat_get_backend_idset()`	`setof integer`	Set of currently active server process numbers (from 1 to the number of active server processes). See usage example in the text
`pg_backend_pid()`	`integer`	Process ID of the server process attached to the current session
`pg_stat_get_backend_pid(integer)`	`integer`	Process ID of the given server process
`pg_stat_get_backend_dbid(integer)`	`oid`	Database ID of the given server process
`pg_stat_get_backend_userid(integer)`	`oid`	User ID of the given server process
`pg_stat_get_backend_activity(integer)`	`text`	Active command of the given server process, but only if the current user is a superuser or the same user as that of the session being queried (and stats_command_string is on)

pg_stat_get_backend_waiting(integer)	boolean	True if the given server process is waiting for a lock, but only if the current user is a superuser or the same user as that of the session being queried (and stats_command_string is on)
pg_stat_get_backend_activity_start(integer)	timestamp with time zone	The time at which the given server process' currently executing query was started, but only if the current user is a superuser or the same user as that of the session being queried (and stats_command_string is on)
pg_stat_get_backend_start(integer)	timestamp with time zone	The time at which the given server process was started, or null if the current user is not a superuser nor the same user as that of the session being queried
pg_stat_get_backend_client_addr(integer)	inet	The IP address of the client connected to the given server process. Null if the connection is over a Unix domain socket. Also null if the current user is not a superuser nor the same user as that of the session being queried

`pg_stat_get_backend_client_port(integer)`	`integer`	The IP port number of the client connected to the given server process. -1 if the connection is over a Unix domain socket. Null if the current user is not a superuser nor the same user as that of the session being queried
`pg_stat_reset()`	`boolean`	Reset all block-level and row-level statistics to zero

Table 12.2: Statistics Access Functions

> **Note:** `blocks_fetched` minus `blocks_hit` gives the number of kernel `read()` calls issued for the table, index, or database; but the actual number of physical reads is usually lower due to kernel-level buffering.

The function `pg_stat_get_backend_idset` provides a convenient way to generate one row for each active server process. For example, to show the PIDs and current queries of all server processes:

```
SELECT pg_stat_get_backend_pid(s.backendid) AS procpid,
       pg_stat_get_backend_activity(s.backendid) AS current_query
    FROM (SELECT pg_stat_get_backend_idset() AS backendid) AS s;
```

12.3 Viewing Locks

Another useful tool for monitoring database activity is the `pg_locks` system table. It allows the database administrator to view information about the outstanding locks in the lock manager. For example, this capability can be used to:

- View all the locks currently outstanding, all the locks on relations in a particular database, all the locks on a particular relation, or all the locks held by a particular PostgreSQL session.

- Determine the relation in the current database with the most ungranted locks (which might be a source of contention among database clients).

- Determine the effect of lock contention on overall database performance, as well as the extent to which contention varies with overall database traffic.

Details of the `pg_locks` view appear in `pg_locks`. For more information on locking and managing concurrency with PostgreSQL, refer to Volume 1, Chapter 10 *Concurrency Control*.

12.4 Dynamic Tracing

PostgreSQL provides facilities to support dynamic tracing of the database server. This allows an external utility to be called at specific points in the code and thereby trace execution. Currently, this facility is primarily intended for use by database developers, as it requires substantial familiarity with the code.

A number of trace points, often called probes, are already inserted into the source code. By default these probes are disabled, and the user needs to explicitly tell the configure script to make the probes available in PostgreSQL.

Currently, only the DTrace utility is supported, which is only available on Solaris Express and Solaris 10+. It is expected that DTrace will be available in the future on FreeBSD and Mac OS X. Supporting other dynamic tracing utilities is theoretically possible by changing the definitions for the PG_TRACE macros in 'src/include/pg_trace.h'.

12.4.1 Compiling for Dynamic Tracing

By default, trace points are disabled, so you will need to explicitly tell the configure script to make the probes available in PostgreSQL. To include DTrace support specify --enable-dtrace to configure. See Section 1.5 *Installation Procedure*, page 9 for further information.

12.4.2 Built-in Trace Points

A few standard trace points are provided in the source code (of course, more can be added as needed for a particular problem). These are shown in Table 12.3.

NAME	PARAMETERS	OVERVIEW
transaction__start	(int transactionId)	The start of a new transaction.
transaction__commit	(int transactionId)	The successful completion of a transaction.
transaction__abort	(int transactionId)	The unsuccessful completion of a transaction.
lwlock__acquire	(int lockid, int mode)	An LWLock has been acquired.
lwlock__release	(int lockid, int mode)	An LWLock has been released.
lwlock__startwait	(int lockid, int mode)	An LWLock was not immediately available and a backend has begun to wait for the lock to become available.
lwlock__endwait	(int lockid, int mode)	A backend has been released from its wait for an LWLock.
lwlock__condacquire	(int lockid, int mode)	An LWLock was successfully acquired when the caller specified no waiting.
lwlock__condacquire__fail	(int lockid, int mode)	An LWLock was not successfully acquired when the caller specified no waiting.
lock__startwait	(int locktag_field2, int lockmode)	A request for a heavyweight lock (lmgr lock) has begun to wait because the lock is not available.
lock__endwait	(int locktag_field2, int lockmode)	A request for a heavyweight lock (lmgr lock) has finished waiting (i.e., has acquired the lock).

Table 12.3: Built-in Trace Points

12.4.3 Using Trace Points

The example below shows a DTrace script for analyzing transaction counts on the system, as an alternative to snapshotting pg_stat_database before and after a performance test.

```
#!/usr/sbin/dtrace -qs

postgresql$1:::transaction-start
{
        @start["Start"] = count();
        self->ts  = timestamp;
}


postgresql$1:::transaction-abort
{
        @abort["Abort"] = count();
}


postgresql$1:::transaction-commit
/self->ts/
{
        @commit["Commit"] = count();
        @time["Total time (ns)"] = sum(timestamp - self->ts);
        self->ts=0;
}
```

Note how the double underline in trace point names needs to be replaced by a hyphen when using D script. When executed, the example D script gives output such as:

```
# ./txn_count.d `pgrep -n postgres`
^C

Start                                           71
Commit                                          70
Total time (ns)                          2312105013
```

You should remember that trace programs need to be carefully written and debugged prior to their use, otherwise the trace information collected may be meaningless. In most cases where problems are found it is the instrumentation that is at fault, not the underlying system. When discussing information found using dynamic tracing, be sure to enclose the script used to allow that too to be checked and discussed.

12.4.4 Defining Trace Points

New trace points can be defined within the code wherever the developer desires, though this will require a recompilation.

A trace point can be inserted by using one of the trace macros. These are chosen according to how many variables will be made available for inspection at that trace point. Tracing the occurrence of an event can be achieved with a single line, using just the trace point name, e.g.

```
PG_TRACE (my__new__trace__point);
```

More complex trace points can be provided with one or more variables for inspection by the dynamic tracing utility by using the PG_TRACE*n* macro that corresponds to the number of parameters after the trace point name:

```
PG_TRACE3 (my__complex__event, varX, varY, varZ);
```

The definition of the transaction__start trace point is shown below:

```
static void
StartTransaction(void)
{
    ...

    /*
     * generate a new transaction id
     */
    s->transactionId = GetNewTransactionId(false);

    XactLockTableInsert(s->transactionId);

    PG_TRACE1(transaction__start, s->transactionId);


    ...
}
```

Note how the transaction ID is made available to the dynamic tracing utility.

The dynamic tracing utility may require you to further define these trace points. For example, DTrace requires you to add new probes to the file 'src/backend/utils/probes.d' as shown here:

```
provider postgresql {
    ...
    probe transaction__start(int);
    ...
};
```

You should take care that the data types specified for the probe arguments match the datatypes of the variables used in the PG_TRACE macro. This is not checked at compile time. You can check that your newly added trace point is available by recompiling, then running the new binary, and as root, executing a DTrace command such as:

```
dtrace -l -n transaction-start
```

13 Monitoring Disk Usage

This chapter discusses how to monitor the disk usage of a PostgreSQL database system.

13.1 Determining Disk Usage

Each table has a primary heap disk file where most of the data is stored. If the table has any columns with potentially-wide values, there is also a TOAST file associated with the table, which is used to store values too wide to fit comfortably in the main table (see TOAST (Volume 4)). There will be one index on the TOAST table, if present. There may also be indexes associated with the base table. Each table and index is stored in a separate disk file—possibly more than one file, if the file would exceed one gigabyte. Naming conventions for these files are described in Volume 4, Section 11.1 *Database File Layout*.

You can monitor disk space in three ways: using SQL functions listed in Table 7.48, using VACUUM information, and from the command line using the tools in 'contrib/oid2name'. The SQL functions are the easiest to use and report information about tables, tables with indexes and long value storage (TOAST), databases, and tablespaces.

Using psql on a recently vacuumed or analyzed database, you can issue queries to see the disk usage of any table:

```
SELECT relfilenode, relpages FROM pg_class WHERE relname =
'customer';

relfilenode | relpages
-------------+----------
      16806 |       60
(1 row)
```

Each page is typically 8 kilobytes. (Remember, relpages is only updated by VACUUM, ANALYZE, and a few data definition language (DDL) commands such as CREATE INDEX.) The relfilenode value is of interest if you want to examine the table's disk file directly.

To show the space used by TOAST tables, use a query like the following:

```
SELECT relname, relpages
    FROM pg_class,
        (SELECT reltoastrelid FROM pg_class
         WHERE relname = 'customer') ss
    WHERE oid = ss.reltoastrelid
      OR oid = (SELECT reltoastidxid FROM pg_class
                WHERE oid = ss.reltoastrelid)
    ORDER BY relname;

      relname        | relpages
---------------------+----------
 pg_toast_16806      |        0
```

```
pg_toast_16806_index |          1
```
You can easily display index sizes, too:
```
SELECT c2.relname, c2.relpages
    FROM pg_class c, pg_class c2, pg_index i
    WHERE c.relname = 'customer'
        AND c.oid = i.indrelid
        AND c2.oid = i.indexrelid
    ORDER BY c2.relname;


        relname        | relpages
----------------------+----------
 customer_id_indexdex |      26
```
It is easy to find your largest tables and indexes using this information:
```
SELECT relname, relpages FROM pg_class ORDER BY relpages DESC;


        relname        | relpages
----------------------+----------
 bigtable             |    3290
 customer             |    3144
```
You can also use 'contrib/oid2name' to show disk usage. See 'README.oid2name' in that directory for examples. It includes a script that shows disk usage for each database.

13.2 Disk Full Failure

The most important disk monitoring task of a database administrator is to make sure the disk doesn't grow full. A filled data disk will not result in data corruption, but it may well prevent useful activity from occurring. If the disk holding the WAL files grows full, database server panic and consequent shutdown may occur.

If you cannot free up additional space on the disk by deleting other things, you can move some of the database files to other file systems by making use of tablespaces. See Section 6.6 *Tablespaces*, page 97 for more information about that.

> **Tip:** Some file systems perform badly when they are almost full, so do not wait until the disk is completely full to take action.

If your system supports per-user disk quotas, then the database will naturally be subject to whatever quota is placed on the user the server runs as. Exceeding the quota will have the same bad effects as running out of space entirely.

14 Reliability and the Write-Ahead Log

This chapter explain how the Write-Ahead Log is used to obtain efficient, reliable operation.

14.1 Reliability

Reliability is an important property of any serious database system, and PostgreSQL does everything possible to guarantee reliable operation. One aspect of reliable operation is that all data recorded by a committed transaction should be stored in a nonvolatile area that is safe from power loss, operating system failure, and hardware failure (except failure of the nonvolatile area itself, of course). Successfully writing the data to the computer's permanent storage (disk drive or equivalent) ordinarily meets this requirement. In fact, even if a computer is fatally damaged, if the disk drives survive they can be moved to another computer with similar hardware and all committed transactions will remain intact.

While forcing data periodically to the disk platters might seem like a simple operation, it is not. Because disk drives are dramatically slower than main memory and CPUs, several layers of caching exist between the computer's main memory and the disk platters. First, there is the operating system's buffer cache, which caches frequently requested disk blocks and combines disk writes. Fortunately, all operating systems give applications a way to force writes from the buffer cache to disk, and PostgreSQL uses those features. (See the wal_sync_method parameter to adjust how this is done.)

Next, there may be a cache in the disk drive controller; this is particularly common on RAID controller cards. Some of these caches are *write-through*, meaning writes are passed along to the drive as soon as they arrive. Others are *write-back*, meaning data is passed on to the drive at some later time. Such caches can be a reliability hazard because the memory in the disk controller cache is volatile, and will lose its contents in a power failure. Better controller cards have *battery-backed* caches, meaning the card has a battery that maintains power to the cache in case of system power loss. After power is restored the data will be written to the disk drives.

And finally, most disk drives have caches. Some are write-through while some are write-back, and the same concerns about data loss exist for write-back drive caches as exist for disk controller caches. Consumer-grade IDE drives are particularly likely to contain write-back caches that will not survive a power failure.

When the operating system sends a write request to the disk hardware, there is little it can do to make sure the data has arrived at a truly non-volatile storage area. Rather, it is the administrator's responsibility to be sure that all storage components ensure data integrity. Avoid disk controllers that have non-battery-backed write caches. At the drive level, disable write-back caching if the drive cannot guarantee the data will be written before shutdown.

Another risk of data loss is posed by the disk platter write operations themselves. Disk platters are divided into sectors, commonly 512 bytes each. Every
physical read or write operation processes a whole sector. When a write request
arrives at the drive, it might be for 512 bytes, 1024 bytes, or 8192 bytes, and
the process of writing could fail due to power loss at any time, meaning some of
the 512-byte sectors were written, and others were not. To guard against such
failures, PostgreSQL periodically writes full page images to permanent storage
before modifying the actual page on disk. By doing this, during crash recovery
PostgreSQL can restore partially-written pages. If you have a battery-backed
disk controller or file-system software that prevents partial page writes (e.g.,
ReiserFS 4), you can turn off this page imaging by using the `full_page_writes`
parameter.

14.2 Write-Ahead Logging (WAL)

Write-Ahead Logging (WAL) is a standard approach to transaction logging.
Its detailed description may be found in most (if not all) books about transaction
processing. Briefly, WAL's central concept is that changes to data files (where
tables and indexes reside) must be written only after those changes have been
logged, that is, when log records describing the changes have been flushed to
permanent storage. If we follow this procedure, we do not need to flush data
pages to disk on every transaction commit, because we know that in the event
of a crash we will be able to recover the database using the log: any changes
that have not been applied to the data pages can be redone from the log records.
(This is roll-forward recovery, also known as REDO.)

A major benefit of using WAL is a significantly reduced number of disk writes,
because only the log file needs to be flushed to disk at the time of transaction
commit, rather than every data file changed by the transaction. In multiuser
environments, commits of many transactions may be accomplished with a single
`fsync` of the log file. Furthermore, the log file is written sequentially, and so
the cost of syncing the log is much less than the cost of flushing the data pages.
This is especially true for servers handling many small transactions touching
different parts of the data store.

WAL also makes it possible to support on-line backup and point-in-time recovery, as described in Section 10.3 *Continuous Archiving and Point-In-Time
Recovery (PITR)*, page 135. By archiving the WAL data we can support revert-
ing to any time instant covered by the available WAL data: we simply install a
prior physical backup of the database, and replay the WAL log just as far as the
desired time. What's more, the physical backup doesn't have to be an instan-
taneous snapshot of the database state—if it is made over some period of time,
then replaying the WAL log for that period will fix any internal inconsistencies.

14.3 WAL Configuration

There are several WAL-related configuration parameters that affect database
performance. This section explains their use. Consult Chapter 4 *Server Configuration*, page 45 for general information about setting server configuration
parameters.

Checkpoints are points in the sequence of transactions at which it is guaranteed that the data files have been updated with all information written before
the checkpoint. At checkpoint time, all dirty data pages are flushed to disk and
a special checkpoint record is written to the log file. In the event of a crash, the
crash recovery procedure looks at the latest checkpoint record to determine the
point in the log (known as the redo record) from which it should start the REDO
operation. Any changes made to data files before that point are known to be
already on disk. Hence, after a checkpoint has been made, any log segments
preceding the one containing the redo record are no longer needed and can be
recycled or removed. (When WAL archiving is being done, the log segments
must be archived before being recycled or removed.)

The server's background writer process will automatically perform a checkpoint every so often. A checkpoint is created every `checkpoint_segments` log
segments, or every `checkpoint_timeout` seconds, whichever comes first. The
default settings are 3 segments and 300 seconds respectively. It is also possible
to force a checkpoint by using the SQL command `CHECKPOINT`.

Reducing `checkpoint_segments` and/or `checkpoint_timeout` causes checkpoints to be done more often. This allows faster after-crash recovery (since
less work will need to be redone). However, one must balance this against the
increased cost of flushing dirty data pages more often. If `full_page_writes` is
set (as is the default), there is another factor to consider. To ensure data page
consistency, the first modification of a data page after each checkpoint results
in logging the entire page content. In that case, a smaller checkpoint interval
increases the volume of output to the WAL log, partially negating the goal of
using a smaller interval, and in any case causing more disk I/O.

Checkpoints are fairly expensive, first because they require writing out all currently dirty buffers, and second because they result in extra subsequent WAL
traffic as discussed above. It is therefore wise to set the checkpointing parameters high enough that checkpoints don't happen too often. As a simple sanity
check on your checkpointing parameters, you can set the `checkpoint_warning`
parameter. If checkpoints happen closer together than `checkpoint_warning`
seconds, a message will be output to the server log recommending increasing
`checkpoint_segments`. Occasional appearance of such a message is not cause
for alarm, but if it appears often then the checkpoint control parameters should
be increased. Bulk operations such as large `COPY` transfers may cause a number of such warnings to appear if you have not set `checkpoint_segments` high
enough.

There will be at least one WAL segment file, and will normally not be more
than 2 * `checkpoint_segments` + 1 files. Each segment file is normally 16 MB
(though this size can be altered when building the server). You can use this
to estimate space requirements for WAL. Ordinarily, when old log segment files
are no longer needed, they are recycled (renamed to become the next segments

in the numbered sequence). If, due to a short-term peak of log output rate, there are more than 2 * `checkpoint_segments` + 1 segment files, the unneeded segment files will be deleted instead of recycled until the system gets back under this limit.

There are two commonly used internal WAL functions: `LogInsert` and `LogFlush`. `LogInsert` is used to place a new record into the WAL buffers in shared memory. If there is no space for the new record, `LogInsert` will have to write (move to kernel cache) a few filled WAL buffers. This is undesirable because `LogInsert` is used on every database low level modification (for example, row insertion) at a time when an exclusive lock is held on affected data pages, so the operation needs to be as fast as possible. What is worse, writing WAL buffers may also force the creation of a new log segment, which takes even more time. Normally, WAL buffers should be written and flushed by a `LogFlush` request, which is made, for the most part, at transaction commit time to ensure that transaction records are flushed to permanent storage. On systems with high log output, `LogFlush` requests may not occur often enough to prevent `LogInsert` from having to do writes. On such systems one should increase the number of WAL buffers by modifying the configuration parameter `wal_buffers`. The default number of WAL buffers is 8. Increasing this value will correspondingly increase shared memory usage. When `full_page_writes` is set and the system is very busy, setting this value higher will help smooth response times during the period immediately following each checkpoint.

The `commit_delay` parameter defines for how many microseconds the server process will sleep after writing a commit record to the log with `LogInsert` but before performing a `LogFlush`. This delay allows other server processes to add their commit records to the log so as to have all of them flushed with a single log sync. No sleep will occur if `fsync` is not enabled, nor if fewer than `commit_siblings` other sessions are currently in active transactions; this avoids sleeping when it's unlikely that any other session will commit soon. Note that on most platforms, the resolution of a sleep request is ten milliseconds, so that any nonzero `commit_delay` setting between 1 and 10000 microseconds would have the same effect. Good values for these parameters are not yet clear; experimentation is encouraged.

The `wal_sync_method` parameter determines how PostgreSQL will ask the kernel to force WAL updates out to disk. All the options should be the same as far as reliability goes, but it's quite platform-specific which one will be the fastest. Note that this parameter is irrelevant if `fsync` has been turned off.

Enabling the `wal_debug` configuration parameter (provided that PostgreSQL has been compiled with support for it) will result in each `LogInsert` and `LogFlush` WAL call being logged to the server log. This option may be replaced by a more general mechanism in the future.

14.4 WAL Internals

WAL is automatically enabled; no action is required from the administrator except ensuring that the disk-space requirements for the WAL logs are met, and that any necessary tuning is done (see Section 14.3 *WAL Configuration*, page 173).

WAL logs are stored in the directory 'pg_xlog' under the data directory, as a set of segment files, normally each 16 MB in size. Each segment is divided into pages, normally 8 kB each. The log record headers are described in 'access/xlog.h'; the record content is dependent on the type of event that is being logged. Segment files are given ever-increasing numbers as names, starting at '000000010000000000000000'. The numbers do not wrap, at present, but it should take a very very long time to exhaust the available stock of numbers.

It is of advantage if the log is located on another disk than the main database files. This may be achieved by moving the directory 'pg_xlog' to another location (while the server is shut down, of course) and creating a symbolic link from the original location in the main data directory to the new location.

The aim of WAL, to ensure that the log is written before database records are altered, may be subverted by disk drives that falsely report a successful write to the kernel, when in fact they have only cached the data and not yet stored it on the disk. A power failure in such a situation may still lead to irrecoverable data corruption. Administrators should try to ensure that disks holding PostgreSQL's WAL log files do not make such false reports.

After a checkpoint has been made and the log flushed, the checkpoint's position is saved in the file 'pg_control'. Therefore, when recovery is to be done, the server first reads 'pg_control' and then the checkpoint record; then it performs the REDO operation by scanning forward from the log position indicated in the checkpoint record. Because the entire content of data pages is saved in the log on the first page modification after a checkpoint, all pages changed since the checkpoint will be restored to a consistent state.

To deal with the case where 'pg_control' is corrupted, we should support the possibility of scanning existing log segments in reverse order—newest to oldest—in order to find the latest checkpoint. This has not been implemented yet. 'pg_control' is small enough (less than one disk page) that it is not subject to partial-write problems, and as of this writing there have been no reports of database failures due solely to inability to read 'pg_control' itself. So while it is theoretically a weak spot, 'pg_control' does not seem to be a problem in practice.

15 Regression Tests

The regression tests are a comprehensive set of tests for the SQL implementation in PostgreSQL. They test standard SQL operations as well as the extended capabilities of PostgreSQL.

15.1 Running the Tests

The regression tests can be run against an already installed and running server, or using a temporary installation within the build tree. Furthermore, there is a "parallel" and a "sequential" mode for running the tests. The sequential method runs each test script in turn, whereas the parallel method starts up multiple server processes to run groups of tests in parallel. Parallel testing gives confidence that interprocess communication and locking are working correctly. For historical reasons, the sequential test is usually run against an existing installation and the parallel method against a temporary installation, but there are no technical reasons for this.

To run the regression tests after building but before installation, type

```
gmake check
```

in the top-level directory. (Or you can change to 'src/test/regress' and run the command there.) This will first build several auxiliary files, such as some sample user-defined trigger functions, and then run the test driver script. At the end you should see something like

```
======================
All 100 tests passed.
======================
```

or otherwise a note about which tests failed. See Section 15.2 *Test Evaluation*, page 179 below before assuming that a "failure" represents a serious problem.

Because this test method runs a temporary server, it will not work when you are the root user (since the server will not start as root). If you already did the build as root, you do not have to start all over. Instead, make the regression test directory writable by some other user, log in as that user, and restart the tests. For example

```
root# chmod -R a+w src/test/regress
root# chmod -R a+w contrib/spi
root# su - joeuser
joeuser$ cd top-level build directory
joeuser$ gmake check
```

(The only possible "security risk" here is that other users might be able to alter the regression test results behind your back. Use common sense when managing user permissions.)

Alternatively, run the tests after installation.

If you have configured PostgreSQL to install into a location where an older PostgreSQL installation already exists, and you perform gmake check before installing the new version, you may find that the tests fail because the new programs try to use the already-installed shared libraries. (Typical symptoms are complaints about undefined symbols.) If you wish to run the tests before overwriting the old installation, you'll need to build with configure --disable-rpath. It is not recommended that you use this option for the final installation, however.

The parallel regression test starts quite a few processes under your user ID. Presently, the maximum concurrency is twenty parallel test scripts, which means forty processes: there's a server process and a psql process for each test script. So if your system enforces a per-user limit on the number of processes, make sure this limit is at least fifty or so, else you may get random-seeming failures in the parallel test. If you are not in a position to raise the limit, you can cut down the degree of parallelism by setting the MAX_CONNECTIONS parameter. For example,

        gmake MAX_CONNECTIONS=10 check

runs no more than ten tests concurrently.

To run the tests after installation (see Chapter 1 *Installation Instructions*, page 5), initialize a data area and start the server, as explained in Chapter 3 *Operating System Environment*, page 27, then type

        gmake installcheck

or for a parallel test

        gmake installcheck-parallel

The tests will expect to contact the server at the local host and the default port number, unless directed otherwise by PGHOST and PGPORT environment variables.

The source distribution also contains regression tests for the optional procedural languages and for some of the 'contrib' modules. At present, these tests can be used only against an already-installed server. To run the tests for all procedural languages that have been built and installed, change to the 'src/pl' directory of the build tree and type

        gmake installcheck

You can also do this in any of the subdirectories of 'src/pl' to run tests for just one procedural language. To run the tests for all 'contrib' modules that have them, change to the 'contrib' directory of the build tree and type

        gmake installcheck

The 'contrib' modules must have been built and installed first. You can also do this in a subdirectory of 'contrib' to run the tests for just one module.

15.2 Test Evaluation

Some properly installed and fully functional PostgreSQL installations can "fail" some of these regression tests due to platform-specific artifacts such as varying floating-point representation and message wording. The tests are currently evaluated using a simple diff comparison against the outputs generated on a reference system, so the results are sensitive to small system differences. When a test is reported as "failed", always examine the differences between expected and actual results; you may well find that the differences are not significant. Nonetheless, we still strive to maintain accurate reference files across all supported platforms, so it can be expected that all tests pass.

The actual outputs of the regression tests are in files in the 'src/test/regress/results' directory. The test script uses diff to compare each output file against the reference outputs stored in the 'src/test/regress/expected' directory. Any differences are saved for your inspection in 'src/test/regress/regression.diffs'. (Or you can run diff yourself, if you prefer.)

If for some reason a particular platform generates a "failure" for a given test, but inspection of the output convinces you that the result is valid, you can add a new comparison file to silence the failure report in future test runs. See Section 15.3 *Variant Comparison Files*, page 181 for details.

15.2.1 Error message differences

Some of the regression tests involve intentional invalid input values. Error messages can come from either the PostgreSQL code or from the host platform system routines. In the latter case, the messages may vary between platforms, but should reflect similar information. These differences in messages will result in a "failed" regression test that can be validated by inspection.

15.2.2 Locale differences

If you run the tests against an already-installed server that was initialized with a collation-order locale other than C, then there may be differences due to sort order and follow-up failures. The regression test suite is set up to handle this problem by providing alternative result files that together are known to handle a large number of locales.

15.2.3 Date and time differences

Most of the date and time results are dependent on the time zone environment. The reference files are generated for time zone PST8PDT (Berkeley, California), and there will be apparent failures if the tests are not run with that time zone setting. The regression test driver sets environment variable PGTZ to PST8PDT, which normally ensures proper results.

15.2.4 Floating-point differences

Some of the tests involve computing 64-bit floating-point numbers (double precision) from table columns. Differences in results involving mathematical functions of double precision columns have been observed. The float8 and geometry tests are particularly prone to small differences across platforms, or even with different compiler optimization options. Human eyeball comparison is needed to determine the real significance of these differences which are usually 10 places to the right of the decimal point.

Some systems display minus zero as -0, while others just show 0.

Some systems signal errors from pow() and exp() differently from the mechanism expected by the current PostgreSQL code.

15.2.5 Row ordering differences

You might see differences in which the same rows are output in a different order than what appears in the expected file. In most cases this is not, strictly speaking, a bug. Most of the regression test scripts are not so pedantic as to use an ORDER BY for every single SELECT, and so their result row orderings are not well-defined according to the letter of the SQL specification. In practice, since we are looking at the same queries being executed on the same data by the same software, we usually get the same result ordering on all platforms, and so the lack of ORDER BY isn't a problem. Some queries do exhibit cross-platform ordering differences, however. When testing against an already-installed server, ordering differences can also be caused by non-C locale settings or non-default parameter settings, such as custom values of work_mem or the planner cost parameters.

Therefore, if you see an ordering difference, it's not something to worry about, unless the query does have an ORDER BY that your result is violating. But please report it anyway, so that we can add an ORDER BY to that particular query and thereby eliminate the bogus "failure" in future releases.

You might wonder why we don't order all the regression test queries explicitly to get rid of this issue once and for all. The reason is that that would make the regression tests less useful, not more, since they'd tend to exercise query plan types that produce ordered results to the exclusion of those that don't.

15.2.6 Insufficient stack depth

If the errors test results in a server crash at the select infinite_recurse() command, it means that the platform's limit on process stack size is smaller than the max_stack_depth parameter indicates. This can be fixed by running the server under a higher stack size limit (4MB is recommended with the default value of max_stack_depth). If you are unable to do that, an alternative is to reduce the value of max_stack_depth.

15.2.7 The random test

The random test script is intended to produce random results. In rare cases, this causes the random regression test to fail. Typing

```
diff results/random.out expected/random.out
```

should produce only one or a few lines of differences. You need not worry unless the random test fails repeatedly.

15.3 Variant Comparison Files

Since some of the tests inherently produce environment-dependent results, we have provided ways to specify alternative "expected" result files. Each regression test can have several comparison files showing possible results on different platforms. There are two independent mechanisms for determining which comparison file is used for each test.

The first mechanism allows comparison files to be selected for specific platforms. There is a mapping file, 'src/test/regress/resultmap', that defines which comparison file to use for each platform. To eliminate bogus test "failures" for a particular platform, you first choose or make a variant result file, and then add a line to the 'resultmap' file.

Each line in the mapping file is of the form

```
testname/platformpattern=comparisonfilename
```

The test name is just the name of the particular regression test module. The platform pattern is a pattern in the style of the Unix tool expr (that is, a regular expression with an implicit ^ anchor at the start). It is matched against the platform name as printed by config.guess. The comparison file name is the base name of the substitute result comparison file.

For example: some systems interpret very small floating-point values as zero, rather than reporting an underflow error. This causes a few differences in the 'float8' regression test. Therefore, we provide a variant comparison file, 'float8-small-is-zero.out', which includes the results to be expected on these systems. To silence the bogus "failure" message on OpenBSD platforms, 'resultmap' includes

```
float8/i.86-.*-openbsd=float8-small-is-zero
```

which will trigger on any machine for which the output of config.guess matches i.86-.*-openbsd. Other lines in 'resultmap' select the variant comparison file for other platforms where it's appropriate.

The second selection mechanism for variant comparison files is much more automatic: it simply uses the "best match" among several supplied comparison files. The regression test driver script considers both the standard comparison file for a test, *testname*.out, and variant files named *testname_digit*.out (where the *digit* is any single digit 0-9). If any such file is an exact match, the test is considered to pass; otherwise, the one that generates the shortest diff is used to create the failure report. (If 'resultmap' includes an entry for the particular test, then the base *testname* is the substitute name given in 'resultmap'.)

For example, for the `char` test, the comparison file 'char.out' contains results that are expected in the C and POSIX locales, while the file 'char_1.out' contains results sorted as they appear in many other locales.

The best-match mechanism was devised to cope with locale-dependent results, but it can be used in any situation where the test results cannot be predicted easily from the platform name alone. A limitation of this mechanism is that the test driver cannot tell which variant is actually "correct" for the current environment; it will just pick the variant that seems to work best. Therefore it is safest to use this mechanism only for variant results that you are willing to consider equally valid in all contexts.

amazon.co.uk

Invoice for
Your order of 15 September, 2009
Order ID 203-0563312-4778766
Invoice number DC6GGPpgR
Invoice date 16 September, 2009

Billing Address
Keith Brailey
1 Brockley Close
Church Fenton
Taddcaster, North Yorkshire LS24 9RB
United Kingdom

Shipping Address
Keith Brailey
1 Brockley Close
Church Fenton
Taddcaster, North Yorkshire LS24 9RB
United Kingdom

Qty.	Item	Bin		Our Price (excl. VAT)	VAT Rate	Total Price
1	**The PostgreSQL Reference Manual Volume 3: Server Administration Guide** Paperback. The PostgreSQL Global Development Group. 0954612043	(** P-1-A72D160 **)		£10.49	0%	£10.49

Conversion rate - £1.00 : EUR 1.14

Shipping charges		£0.00	0%	£0.00
Subtotal (excl. VAT) 0%				£10.49
Total VAT				£0.00
Total				£10.49

We've sent this portion of your order separately at no extra charge to give you the speediest service possible. The other items in your order are shipping separately, and your total postage and packing charges for this order will not exceed the amount we originally charged.

You can always check the status of your orders or change your account
details from the "Your Account" link at the top of each page on our site.

Thinking of returning an item? PLEASE USE OUR ON-LINE RETURNS SUPPORT CENTRE.

Our Returns Support Centre (www.amazon.co.uk/returns-support) will guide you through our Returns Policy
and provide you with a printable personalised return label. Please have your order number ready (you
can find it next to your order summary, above). Our Returns Policy does not affect your statutory rights.

Thank you for shopping at Amazon.co.uk!

Amazon EU S.à r.l; 5, Rue Plaetis, L - 2338 Luxembourg
VAT number : GB727255821

Please note - this is not a returns address - for returns - please see above for details of our online returns cent

54

Books from the publisher

Network Theory publishes books about free software under free documentation licenses. Our current catalogue includes the following titles:

- **PostgreSQL Reference Manual: Volume 1** (ISBN 0-9546120-2-7) $49.95 (£32.00)

  This manual documents the SQL language and commands of PostgreSQL. For each copy of this manual sold, $1 is donated to the PostgreSQL project.

- **PostgreSQL Reference Manual: Volume 2** (ISBN 0-9546120-3-5) $34.95 (£19.95)

  This manual documents the client and server programming interfaces of PostgreSQL. For each copy of this manual sold, $1 is donated to the PostgreSQL project.

- **PostgreSQL Reference Manual: Volume 3** (ISBN 0-9546120-4-3) $24.95 (£13.95)

  This manual is a guide to the configuration and maintenance of PostgreSQL database servers. For each copy of this manual sold, $1 is donated to the PostgreSQL project.

- **GNU Bash Reference Manual** by Chet Ramey and Brian Fox (ISBN 0-9541617-7-7) $29.95 (£19.95)

  This manual is the definitive reference for GNU Bash, the standard GNU command-line interpreter. GNU Bash is a complete implementation of the POSIX.2 Bourne shell specification, with additional features from the C-shell and Korn shell. For each copy of this manual sold, $1 is donated to the Free Software Foundation.

- **Version Management with CVS** by Per Cederqvist et al. (ISBN 0-9541617-1-8) $29.95 (£19.95)

  This manual describes how to use CVS, the concurrent versioning system— one of the most widely-used source-code management systems available today. The manual provides tutorial examples for new users of CVS, as well as the definitive reference documentation for every CVS command and configuration option.

- **Comparing and Merging Files with GNU diff and patch** by David MacKenzie, Paul Eggert, and Richard Stallman (ISBN 0-9541617-5-0) $19.95 (£12.95)

  This manual describes how to compare and merge files using GNU diff and patch. It includes an extensive tutorial that guides the reader through all the options of the diff and patch commands. For each copy of this manual sold, $1 is donated to the Free Software Foundation.

- **An Introduction to GCC** by Brian J. Gough, foreword by Richard M. Stallman. (ISBN 0-9541617-9-3) $19.95 (£12.95)

  This manual provides a tutorial introduction to the GNU C and C++ compilers, gcc and g++. Many books teach the C and C++ languages, but this book explains how to use the compiler itself. Based on years of observation of questions posted on mailing lists, it guides the reader straight to the important options of GCC.

- **An Introduction to Python** by Guido van Rossum and Fred L. Drake, Jr. (ISBN 0-9541617-6-9) $19.95 (£12.95)

  This tutorial provides an introduction to Python, an easy to learn object oriented programming language. For each copy of this manual sold, $1 is donated to the Python Software Foundation.

- **Python Language Reference Manual** by Guido van Rossum and Fred L. Drake, Jr. (ISBN 0-9541617-8-5) $19.95 (£12.95)

  This manual is the official reference for the Python language itself. It describes the syntax of Python and its built-in datatypes in depth, This manual is suitable for readers who need to be familiar with the details and rules of the Python language and its object system. For each copy of this manual sold, $1 is donated to the Python Software Foundation.

- **GNU Octave Manual** by John W. Eaton (ISBN 0-9541617-2-6) $29.99 (£19.99)

  This manual is the definitive guide to GNU Octave, an interactive environment for numerical computation with matrices and vectors. For each copy sold $1 is donated to the GNU Octave Development Fund.

- **GNU Scientific Library Reference Manual—Revised Second Edition** by M. Galassi, et al (ISBN 0-9541617-3-4) $39.99 (£24.99)

  This reference manual is the definitive guide to the GNU Scientific Library (GSL), a numerical library for C and C++ programmers. The manual documents over 1,000 mathematical routines needed for solving problems in science and engineering. All the money raised from the sale of this book supports the development of the GNU Scientific Library.

- **An Introduction to R** by W.N. Venables, D.M. Smith and the R Development Core Team (ISBN 0-9541617-4-2) $19.95 (£12.95)

  This tutorial manual provides a comprehensive introduction to GNU R, a free software package for statistical computing and graphics.

- **The R Reference Manual—Base Package (Volumes 1 & 2)** by the R Development Core Team (ISBN 0-9546120-0-0 and 0-9546120-1-9) $69.95 each (£39.95 each)

These volumes are the complete reference manual for the base package of GNU R, a free software environment for statistical computing and graphics. The main commands of the base package of R are described in volume one, while the other functions (such as graphics) are described in volume two. For each set of manuals sold, $10 is donated to the R Foundation.

All titles are available for order from bookstores worldwide.

Sales of the manuals fund the development of more free software and documentation.

For details, visit the website http://www.network-theory.co.uk/

Index

Lightning Source UK Ltd.
Milton Keynes UK
20 August 2009

142899UK00001B/313/A

9 780954 612047